P9-DGY-054

THE BEAUTY OF THE BEAST

Other Books by Geoffrey Bellman

Your Signature Path

Getting Things Done When You Are Not in Charge

The Consultant's Calling

The Quest for Staff Leadership

THE BEAUTY OF THE BEAST

Breathing New Life into Organizations

GEOFFREY M. BELLMAN

BK

BERRETT-KOEHLER PUBLISHERS, INC.
San Francisco

Berrett-Koehler Publishers, Inc.
450 Sansome Street, Suite 1200
San Francisco, CA 94111-3320
Tel: (415) 288-0260 Fax: (415) 362-2512 www.bkconnection.com

Ordering Information

Quantity sales. Special discounts are available on quantity purchases by corporations, associations, and others. For details, contact the "Special Sales Department" at the Berrett-Koehler address above.

Individual sales. Berrett-Koehler publications are available through most bookstores. They can also be ordered direct from Berrett-Koehler:
Tel: (800) 929-2929; Fax: (802) 864-7626; www.bkconnection.com

Orders for college textbook/course adoption use. Please contact Berrett-Koehler:
Tel: (800) 929-2929; Fax: (802) 864-7626.

Orders by U.S. trade bookstores and wholesalers. Please contact Publishers Group West, 1700 Fourth Street, Berkeley, CA 94710. Tel: (510) 528-1444; Fax: (510) 528-3444.

Printed in the United States of America
Printed on acid-free and recycled paper that is composed of 85% recovered fiber, including 10% post consumer waste.

Library of Congress Cataloging-in-Publication Data

Bellman, Geoffrey M., 1938–
The beauty of the beast : breathing new life into organizations / Geoffrey Bellman.
p. cm.
Includes bibliographical references and index.
ISBN 1-57675-093-0 (alk. paper)
1. Organization. 2. Management. I. Title.

HD31 .B3784 2000
658.4'06--dc21

99-058681

First Edition
06 05 04 03 02 01 00 10 9 8 7 6 5 4 3 2 1

Interior Design/Art: Mendocino Graphics
Proofreading: Marla Greenway
Editing: Elinor Lindheimer
Indexing: Paula C. Durbin-Westby
Production: Linda Jupiter, Jupiter Productions

To the Woodlands Group

Forrest and Betty Belcher,
Mac and Minette McCullough,
Ned and Margy Herrmann, Mavis Wilson,
Boyce and Jeannie Appel,
Pat McLagan, Frank and Susie Basler,
Steve Cohen, Paul and Kris Anne Gustavson,
Peggy and Buddy Hutcheson,
Nancy Kuhn, Carlene and Bruce Reinhart,
Bill Synder, Bob and Mary Stump,
and Sheila Kelly.

With gratitude for our years together,
seeking the beauty.

Table of Contents

Preface		ix
Part I	**Facing the Beast**	1
Chapter 1	Hating and Loving Organizations	3
Chapter 2	Accepting Organizations for What They Are	13
Chapter 3	Creating a Bureaucracy to Curse	21
Part II	**Searching for the Beauty**	35
Chapter 4	Essential Questions for Organizations	41
Chapter 5	Aspiring to Life	53
Chapter 6	Signs of Life in Your Organization	63
Part III	**Finding Beauty Within the Beast**	71
Chapter 7	The Reach for Renewal	75
Chapter 8	The Roots of Renewal	85
Chapter 9	The Response to Renewal	95
Chapter 10	The Realities of Renewal	105

Part IV Renewing Organizations, Groups, and Individuals 123

Chapter 11 Renewing a Large Organization 125

Chapter 12 Bringing Work Groups to Life 135

Chapter 13 Praticing Renewal Daily 143

Conclusion: The Choices We Make 153

Related Resources 157

Index 159

About the Author 165

Preface

"First, we shape our structures. Then, our structures shape us."
—Winston Churchill

Organizations are the world's 21st-century dilemma. They are magnificent and mad, wonderful and wretched, crazy and compelling. They make so little, and so much, sense. Never before has humankind been able to bring together so many global resources within common form and purpose. Our ability to create organizations exceeds our ability to control them; they have power beyond imagining.

Organizations are a personal dilemma as well. We rely on them and rail against them. They promise us gratification; we promise to pay within ninety days. They lend us their resources in return for our loyalty. We search for our meaning through them as their suppliers, customers, workers, citizens, beneficiaries, and victims. We live in hope and fear of the consequences of their actions. We are living a science fiction take: "We have created a monster!" The monster may be called agency, or government, or health care, or education, or corporation. We all live and work around these beasts—all of them, but especially corporations because of their accelerating power in the transformation of the global marketplace.

This book's title alludes to the fairy tale in which a merchant gives his pure-hearted daughter, Belle, to the Beast in exchange for his own life. Belle, despite her initial horror, chooses to look for the best in the Beast and gradually finds it. In fact, she finds fulfillment where she at first felt revulsion. This book is for the Belle in each of us, encouraging us to face and find life where we stand, to choose in this moment to create the next. By choosing, we breathe the new life into organizations that we all so urgently need.

Who This Book Is For

Many of us are as intrigued with the potential of organizations as we are disturbed with the reality; we are drawn into relationships with these bureaucratic beasts out of attraction as well as necessity. Millions of us join our personal purpose with organizational purpose, hoping for the best and making the most of this uneasy marriage . . . for better or for worse, for rich or for poor, in sickness and in health. We live in the struggle to find meaning within structures that were not built with us in mind.

Many of us recognize how essential organizations are to what we have achieved and what we will become; we see the immense potential they represent. We know they figure in the future of life on this planet. We are part of a highly educated workforce that each day steps into organizations that have not caught up with what we have learned about ourselves. We seek our actualization in organizations put together for other purposes; we feel our schizophrenia as our minds and hearts proclaim the possibilities and our organizations proclaim the limitations. We are seeing more attempts at creating productive organizations filled with human accomplishment and spirit, but there is so far to go. This book is for people who know this line of thinking and want to continue it.

Why Read This Book

We need new perspectives on what organizations are for and how to change them. Our organizational models of immediate gratification for the few are not working for the many. There must be ways of working that honor long-term aspirations and fulfillment. We need grand expectations, so big they cannot be realized in our lifetimes. We need to awaken to and work toward these immense purposes, measuring our progress toward fine aspirations for tomorrow—rather than continually gratifying ourselves today.

This book helps you step back from organizations to ask: Why do we keep creating these creatures that fall so far short of our dreams for them? What is our role in doing this? And the book helps you move in close to consider why you give so much of your life to these occasionally exhilarating and often frustrating beasts.

This book helps you imagine what people can do together and how they might do it. It engages you in thinking about what you could do at work, and offers you ideas on how to do it. It guides you in a personal and organizational exploration in search of purpose, contribution, community, and identity. Its many questions open you to answers you have not yet considered, while its content will inspire your daily work. It's a book to be read frequently over time, allowing its ideas to soak into your thoughts and actions. This book helps you embrace the organizational world as it is while working hard to change it.

How This Book Is Structured

As the title suggests, the organization is beauty *and* beast, not separate but joined within one form. This creates a necessary inner tension, which the organization is intent on resolving. The book is about using that tension to propel the organization forward toward its dreams while staying rooted in its reality.

Part One declares the beastly side of organization and asks us to face and, eventually, perhaps even embrace it. This part helps us acknowledge what we hate and love about these creatures, as well as what we gain and lose in the process. We will see how needs for achievement, stature, and predictability result in our complex bureaucracies. We come to a greater understanding of—and respect for—the power of the beast in ourselves. And amid all of the tension and struggle, Part One underlines the reality that organizations in some form are indispensable to a more productive and fulfilled human community.

Part Two begins the search for beauty and life in organizations. It helps us define the organizations and lives we aspire to over the long term; we will begin to seek beauty and life at work. Part Two helps us imagine the organizations we want to create, offering eight aspirations necessary for organizations to live not just next year, but for centuries. It helps us begin looking for answers where they might be found, rather than continuing to search in places where no answers are available. And since there are many encouraging signs of life in our organizations; a few of them are offered here.

Part Three is about the choices that bind the beauty and the beast of the organization together. It helps us recognize the necessary tension and vitality in this marriage and offers twenty renewal assertions holding organizations together for a better future. These assertions help us breathe new life into the work we are now doing—refreshing our meetings, reformulating our discussions, renewing our organizations.

Part Four offers three applications of renewal of life: within a large organization, within a work team, and within you, the reader of this book. These examples are intended to launch us toward our own aspirations, to put our ideas into practice.

Briefly, this book is about facing the organizational beast (Part One), searching for the beauty we aspire to (Part Two), and making the daily choices that renew organizations and ourselves (Part Three). It's about committing to the work world as it is, discovering what it can be, and delighting in our work of changing it.

Acknowledgments

If the chapters of this book were heavily footnoted, those notes would be longer than the book! The resources section at the end of the book lists a number of writers to whom I am indebted, but by no means all. If you see an idea here that relates to a conversation we have had or something you published, assume that you helped me learn what I've now written as my own.

Six reviewers read this book in a form that only vaguely resembles what you now hold in your hands. They struggled through seventy pages more than you will see; hardly a page of that manuscript did not receive a note from at least one of them. Their comments were profoundly influential and I am deeply grateful. I thank each of them: Stewart Lanier, Jennifer Leigh, Jeff Pym, Sheila Kelly, Frank Basler, and Allan Paulson. Sheila also edited the final draft and helped shape it to what you see—testimony both to her talent and to the strength of our marriage.

This is my third book with Berrett-Koehler and, as I have come to expect, Steve Piersanti and his staff have immersed me in their expertise and care. I am fortunate to be with a publisher—with an organization—that aspires to create what I write about in this book. Thank you all, again!

Over the last four years, I have been part of the Community Consulting Project, a small group of invested citizens that learns about organizations and consulting by working in Seattle's not-for-profit community. My work with voluntary organizations opened my eyes to possibilities for the corporate organizations I have served most of my life. I am grateful for what CCP has given me; I think it shows in these pages.

And lastly, I acknowledge the Woodlands Group; you can find all of their names on the dedication page. This small and voluntary organization has been meeting quarterly for close to twenty-five years. I have attended almost every meeting; you can imagine how important these people and our purposes have become to me. We have learned together about life and work in organizations, and in the process have become a small and loving organization ourselves. Our meetings have become a celebration of our lives, our work in the world, and our little community. This group lives and breathes the aspirations of this book.

Geoff Bellman
Seattle
November, 1999

Part One

Facing the Beast

Most organizations are beastly creatures to live with and guide; they have developed power, energy, and intelligence beyond what most of us ever imagined. Many of us pull away from these beasts, automatically assigning them less humanity and heart. We see their primitive power and we stand back from their threat and unpredictability. Our fears often turn to prejudice; we "know" what an organization is before we experience it. Part One is about facing these beasts, facing the truth of their ugliness, and eventually coming to terms with them. It's about taking the early risks that allow us to learn more about organizations and appreciate them for what they are—rather than what we imagine. We are like Belle in the fairy tale, our lives are at risk and we must choose how we are going to see the Beast before us. And we will make her choice: We will proceed with the belief that there is something deeper here, something to be appreciated, if we open ourselves to it. This is a courageous step full of faith, and we may not be rewarded as Belle was. We may not live happily ever after. After all, what we are living is not a fairy tale.

Organizations are with us and will be with us as long as we humans exist. Face it; face them. Imagine throwing your arms around this huge, powerful, hairy creature you call the organization. . . . Imagine looking it in the eye, knowing it deeply, finding what there is to appreciate. Read this part of the book with the intent of looking deeply. And, while looking at the organization, take a good look at yourself, notice the eyes through which you see organizations. We each use our view of organizations to define and judge them. What is the view you hold?

My view is that the beginning of the beauty we aspire to is here; we just have to see it. The path to the organization we dream about runs through the door of the organization we live in; we must walk it. There is no transporting ourselves to a new and more perfect organizational world. This is it. This is as perfect as worlds come. So we begin here, holding our dreams and living with the reality. Whatever we will do to move ourselves or this organization in the direction of our aspirations will begin right here. This is a hard truth to swallow when we are deep in our disdain for, or hatred of, or revulsion for, an organization. This is not a truth we want to hear. But it is the truth: Face the Beast.

Chapter 1

Hating and Loving Organizations

As with many relationships, ours with organizations varies from problematic to traumatic to romantic to ecstatic . . . but they are seldom static. Pursuing our individual purpose within a larger community can be troublesome, whether we are deciding about working on a team, or going to a family reunion, or choosing our telephone service provider. An array of thoughts, emotions, and questions comes to the fore, provoked by what we might gain or lose through making this commitment. Today's huge organizations incite larger emotions as we become one among millions in their databases. We have more choices than ever before, but we must choose from among the options they offer. "Press the number one on your keypad if you want. . . . " We have less direct influence on forming those options: one hundred television channels and nothing is on. We know the feelings that arise as we try to get what we want from a large organization. We are locked in a close tight dance in which we don't name the tune, don't get to look our partner in the eye, don't get to lead—and it's a rather hairy partner at that! At least it can feel that way.

Or it can be wonderful. Websites that show and tell all you need to know for a purchase without ever leaving home . . . clothing made to fit you . . . information at your fingertips through search engines . . . the handiness of credit cards . . . the cell phone. . . . These are just a few examples of services and products meeting your needs better than before. Large organizations serve us best when they can offer us what we want quickly and conveniently and routinely. The dance can be smooth and satisfying when we name the right tune.

This chapter extends the dance, helping you explore your relationships with organizations, what you get and give in the process. This chart shows what you will be working with:

	Hating	Loving
Help	How Does Hating Organizations Help You?	How Does Loving Organizations Help You?
Harm	How Does Hating Organizations Harm You?	How Does Loving Organizations Harm You?

This two-by-two matrix shows dynamics among hate and love, harm and help; its questions ask you to look into your own experience with organizations. The questions could have been, "How does loving/hating *this* organization help/harm you?" In fact, you may find it useful to read this chapter with a particular organization in mind—one with which you have a long term, or at least interesting, relationship. It could be a company, a school, an agency, a church, a marriage, a scout troop, a political party. The matrix pushes you toward polarities—love<>hate and help<>harm—and encourages you to exaggerate your responses along the way.

Imagine forty people in four teams recreating this matrix, each team moving to a separate quarter of the room to deal with one quadrant with its question. Imagine the teams answering the questions and shouting their answers across the room to each other. That's what happened on an early outing with this matrix, provoking thought, passionate expression, feelings, and hilarity as people reflected on themselves. I want to provoke this kind of expression and energy in you. See, hear, notice what questions you care most about; call out your confluence and contradiction; define your relationship with organizations as you fill the boxes with your answers. Take time to answer the questions now. My bet is you will be intrigued with your answers—and the feelings that accompany them.

After completing the four quadrants:

- Which is the most compelling quadrant for you?
- Where (if at all) are you most clearly aligned?
- Where (if at all) do you see dilemmas?
- What can you say about yourself now that you might not have said before?
- Who would be interested in discussing this with you?

This matrix is a simple way of teasing out the sources of our discontent, and pleasure, with the organizational beasts around us, allowing us to search out the source of our energy for organization work. To aid your exploration, I will make my own trip around the four quadrants. I will share my experience with loving and hating organizations to stimulate your thoughts and feelings.

Love and Help

Large organizations are more fascinating to me today than when I began working with them years ago. I am intrigued by their personalities, their behaviors, their unpredictability. I see them as individuals with many of the same characteristics as people. I love to watch them, participate in them, help build their success, and continue to figure out what "makes them tick." Though I'm convinced they are unfathomable, I continue trying to fathom them.

My fascination with organizations was fed as I left full employment in one to begin consulting to many. From the inside, I had a deeper appreciation of the workings of the organization I was then serving. I also turned its peculiarities into generalizations: What I found wrong with my employer I "knew" was wrong with organizations in general. From the outside, after years of working with hundreds of companies, I see how much they have in common and how much my learning about one is applicable to others. Much of my work has been spreading learning across organizations, assuring each that their problems are not as unique as they might imagine in their more anxious moments.

I still love the anthems and rhythms created when crowds of people, sharing some common purpose and acknowledging roughly the same boundaries, try to do something together. I'm intrigued by how much the donut makers, god worshippers, insurance sellers, ball players, star seekers, steel makers, and salmon savers have in common. They are much more similar than different when I watch them work. Just as people are similar in their outward makeup (arms, legs, language, habits) so organizations seem to work in similar ways regardless of purpose, and I have been privileged to watch all of that—and get paid for watching!

My love for organizations has helped me in numerous ways. First of all, it has fed me for over thirty years. Organizations have fed my mind, heart, and family. Organizations have made me a part of their large purposes; they have put their resources at my disposal. They have given me other people who are also on "my side"; my power in the world has been multiplied through working with them. Working with organizations has allowed me to be influential, and I have made a number of good friends along the way.

Love and Harm

Loving
Harm

My love for organizations causes me to believe in them, to dismiss critics and doubters too early. In the process, I lose the benefit of other perspectives that would help me make better choices. My allegiance to organizations comes with blinders. Other more independent people have drawn back from my willingness to appreciate or ascribe good intentions to these monoliths. In the heat of discussion or resolution of conflicts, I often forget that I am making assumptions about organizations that are different from and no more valid than others' assumptions.

In my life as an organizational observer and player, organizations have given power to me and I have given them a power over me. I have supported their definitions of success in the work we did together. I certainly influenced them, but they decided whether I would be there to influence them. As I gained intimate knowledge of them—especially corporations—I became more like them. They defined their game and I played it. I continually reminded myself of the larger, personal life game I was living, but returning to their halls and meetings year after year affected my independent thinking and choice. I've prided myself on my independence, but I have also fooled myself. My ego, loving the strokes that come with successful organization work, often equates and mistakes that success with human progress.

My work with organizations has usually involved money. I want to assign high motives to organizations that pay me well and often; I have distorted my reality to fit theirs. In addition to keeping me from addressing the needs of worthwhile organizations with no money, my actions say that organizations with money are the most important in the world. How much have I lost in this bargain?

Hate and Harm

I often hate what organizations do, what they do to people, what they do to the world. Years of working with corporations have refined my disgust for what they are capable of doing in the service of control, speed, and greed. Recent times have created companies hugely distorted toward profit. Often stakeholders like the community or suppliers are neglected in favor of immediate returns for the stockholders and management. The profit motive becomes an organizational cancer growing faster and out of proportion to the rest of the corporate body; profit crowds out all other purpose and consumes energy needed for wider corporate health. Traditionally, the church or the state or the military perverted power. Now in our market-driven society it is corporations that abuse the power derived from their amassed wealth.

My fixation on the faults of organizations reduces, or eliminates, any sense of personal responsibility for what they are doing. I separate them from me, make them objects to despise, worthy of my hatred. They are wonderful villains! I diminish and lift myself at their expense. They become smaller, I become larger. I inflate my goodness and their badness. Hating them distorts my views of myself.

Large organizations have the potential to bind human energy in the service of greater good for all of us. They present the possibility of human communities that unite our spirit. They can hold out the promise of widespread fulfillment and happiness. Sometimes I hate them because they fall so far short of this potential—the same reasons I occasionally hate associates, friends, and myself. My expectations of them come from my expectations of myself. Since I hate it when I fall short, I hate it when they fall short. I project onto them what I expect of myself and they don't make it. I am disappointed in them because I am disappointed in myself. . . . And my diatribe against organizations turns on me!

That's how it is for many of us. The words vary, but the melody is the same: We often expect of others what we expect of ourselves. To the extent we are punishing ourselves, we will punish others for similarly perceived shortcomings. To the extent we are accepting of ourselves, we will be more accepting of others. That punishment or acceptance often extends more easily to faceless organizations that are safer to blame than to an individual who might retaliate.

Hate and Help

The organizational failings of my clients are a dependable source of inner turmoil: Can I continue to support organizations that damage the world and its people? To what extent am I selling out? My hatred of their abuses is one source of energy to change them and the world in some small ways. The gap between what they do and could do calls out for action. Organizations are powerful in the world; I have skills useful in changing them. If I want to make a difference, what better place is there for me to act? It makes sense . . . and, I can imagine myself as just what they need—a missionary to the heathens, a breath of fresh air, a light in the darkness. All those fantasies feed my sense of importance to them, to the world, and to myself. Even without the fantasy, the reality of organizational shortcomings and potential helps me act.

Here is some surprising, shadowy help coming out of my difficulties with organizations: With time, my pattern of concerns about organizations have boomeranged. I have considered: Why do I hate these abuses so much? Why am I disturbed again and again over what I see? No one is asking me to hold that concern or emotion. Gradually I am realizing that what I hate in organizations is often what I hate in myself—that part of myself I have yet to come to terms with. With this perspective, I find my intense response to what is going on out there in a particular organization hints at something unresolved within myself. Yes, there truly are problems out there, but the problems inside myself are the more compelling; they affect and distort my views on everything. This unintended, backhanded gift coming from organizations has helped me look into and learn about myself.

Summary

Expectations of myself have been a vital source of energy for the organizational change work I've done over the years. My self-imposed expectations allow me to pursue this work more vigorously. I have helped organizations reach for what I wanted to become myself. For years, I thought that my ideas were complete, that I was complete, and that I was taking that completeness to organizations. I gradually became aware that my energy for my work was an attempt to fill in what I lacked. I needed others to change because I needed to change. That is still true today, but much less than ten years ago. As my acceptance of myself has increased, so has my acceptance of other people and of organizations. Perhaps my experience has something to do with your own:

- How do you project your aspirations and limitations onto organizations?
- Of all that is there, what are you choosing to see?
- How did your early life prepare you to see organizations as you do?
- What is the agenda you bring to each organization you work with?

We do not control the organizations we work with and we are only with them part of the time. We have more control over ourselves, and we are with ourselves constantly. This suggests that any efforts at changing an organization might start with us also. Return to the opening matrix for this chapter and replace one word: Replace "organizations" with "myself." My work with organizations begins with myself.

The choice to begin our work on organizations with ourselves is a hard one, and usually not reinforced by the people around us. But let's face it, the approach of placing all the blame and responsibility on organizations has not made people any happier. Millions of people have not become more fulfilled by declaring that someone or something else is responsible for their anger and emptiness. Then, when you take responsibility for your life, you often have to work with others who still lay all of the responsibility on organizations. This does not make your choice any easier. Perhaps you could engage them in an exploration of what they gain and lose in their own hating and loving of an organization. Perhaps you could figure out a few actions you could take together that would more likely bring all of you a bit more happiness in your work. Pay attention to what they love, to where their passion is, to what brings them to life. That's a peek into the possibilities.

Chapter 2

Accepting Organizations for What They Are

Organizations loom large in our lives. They lift and move us; they feed and drape us; they brand us with their swoops and stripes; they color all that we do. They pool the talents of tens of thousands of people so we can have the drink, music, flight, movie, education, check, or drumstick when we want it and how we want it. They hold out the comfort, clarity, and convenience; the peace, peril, and power; the security, seduction, and satisfaction we are looking for. They offer themselves, their products and services, as if there were nothing in the world more important than meeting our needs. And they serve themselves while serving us.

And we feed them. With every credit card, bus pass, tax payment, welfare check, and Internet transaction, we nourish their lives. Willingly or begrudgingly . . . we affirm their continued existence; we declare our dependence. And of course, we are them. We form their ranks as employees; we make their purpose our own for our best hours each day. And to rest up or escape from our employers, we consider the alternatives offered by other organizations, whether it's a movie at the multiplex, franchise food, or a cruise of the Caribbean. Wherever we turn, there they are with their enlightenment, enticement, and encouragement. Our world offers us choices among organizations, and we'd rather not choose to do without them. The proclamations of individuality, independence, and self sufficiency are lost as we converge on the malls, embracing the latest trend in eyewear, footwear, and four-wheel-drive hardware. Those few people who opt out are notable because they are such an exception—and we act like they are just a little bit crazy.

Imagine a future world without large organizations. Imagine making your clothes, growing your food, heating your home, walking to work. Step back a century and you will find most people in the Western world doing just that. In less than a hundred years, we have shifted our lives from supporting ourselves to relying on large organizations to support us. We are so caught up in the reality of these huge creatures that we cannot imagine a world without them. Look at the labels on your clothing; where does it come from? And this book you are reading? And your telephones? And the carpet, the lamp, the computer? Was your computer keyboard carved from wood by a Vermont craftsman? Hardly. Organizations, many organizations in many countries, cooperated so you could have that keyboard, that carpet, those clothes.

These organizations were created in service to dreams. Behind every organization are the people who imagined it. They created these creatures to multiply and accelerate themselves. Organizations are cauldrons of power, heat, intelligence, intensity, equipment, and emotion. Mysterious in their makeup and behavior, they are a wonder to watch and a challenge to guide. So much of what surrounds us is made possible through the cooperation of millions of people in thousands of organizations around the globe. Somehow, organizations help normal, everyday people combine their work in wonderful ways, resulting in products and services that are exceptional. Not always, but often. (I hear a train in the distance, probably a mile long, leaving Seattle headed east, stacked with containers stuffed with toys or tires or televisions, transferred from ships to flatcars, on their way from the Far East to the East Coast, a sixteen-day journey.)

These large organizations are so much a part of our recent past and present, and increasingly central to our future. Consider the communications revolution now engulfing us, creating unimaginable global transformation, and only possible through the interweaving of talent and technology by huge organizations. As these organizations accelerate along their current trajectory, what might they be two or ten or a hundred generations from now? Will they self-destruct? Will they radically alter in shape and purpose? How will they affect our human evolution? These huge organizations loom large in our future; they are necessary to it; they expand our possibilities; they are a blessing.

And . . .

They are a curse! Organizations often represent the worst of what we can do together. These crazy-making creatures lock people together in mindless structures within rules they don't understand, going places they don't want to go. If someone set out to regularly abuse human talent, spirit, and purpose, they could hardly do better than create some of our organizational structures: corporations, governments, education, social service, churches; no purpose or people are exempt. Sometimes it seems as if we searched centuries for ways of misusing human talent and came up with our authority-worshipping, talent-diminishing, heart-stomping structures. They feed the worst traits of controlling, egotistical leaders, amplifying those traits down through multiple layers of structure. Never have so many capable people produced so much service, profit, product, and stress—with so little fulfillment and happiness. Ancient military models have been refined into machine models and are now becoming even more analytical, precise, and controlling with electronic brains that extend their power further and faster.

Loving Our Dilemmas

There is truth in the blessings and truth in the curses: the spectacle and sterility, the mystery and madness, the continuity and contradiction. The truth of it all intrigues many of us, making organizations irresistible. Whether we are in them as missionaries or mercenaries, many of us love being a part of their huge game. Some of us love helping them recognize a larger purpose beyond this month or this year; we love engaging them in pursuit of their deeper meaning. Or we love to use their power, to bring it to bear on issues important to us. Others of us love to beat up on them, to use them to work out our own issues with power. Our years and years of working in them feed our needs for learning, challenge, recognition, accomplishment, power, stature, and contribution. At least, that is the possibility.

Our hopes for organizations became more vivid and compelling in the latter part of the twentieth century. More people began to see work organizations as a place to seek meaning and create happiness. They saw the possibility that these organizations could succeed and could support the success of the people in and around them: workers, suppliers, customers, families, stockholders, communities, and society. All that is indeed possible—but not in most organizations at this moment. What organizations are now is far short of what they can be. Eventually, it is all possible that our hopes will be realized. It may take lifetimes, but it is possible.

As Winston Churchill said, "First, we shape our structures. Then, our structures shape us." Our forefathers shaped these structures of education, government, the marketplace, religion, over the centuries, and they have shaped us in return. We ask people to fit themselves into these old structures, to sit in their assigned places. But an old structure often lacks the space to accommodate its human occupants. People step into their work spaces and it's not long before they are pushing out at the walls. Or they move in and fully occupy the roles they have been assigned, acquiescing to role expectations that they not be themselves while at work. We are more aware of these kinds of problems today than ever before.

Our highly educated workforce and the tumultuous change in organizations combine to create work dissatisfaction unique to this age. People's expectations of fulfillment are higher than ever before. At the same time, many feel betrayed by large organizations—and we do not know what to do about it. Everybody has an opinion and nobody knows; the villains are everywhere and nowhere. Today it's management; tomorrow it's the union. Today it's the new administration; tomorrow it's apathetic citizens. Or it's elected officials . . . and then the bureaucracy. Or it's you . . . no, maybe it's me. Breaking our patterns of finding fault and blaming allows us to see that the answers we need go beyond the battles we wage. The solutions lie more in reforming organizations than in resolving individual conflicts. Even short-term questions have long-term answers.

Those of us who have been working to reform organizations know something about asking questions, about stepping outside of our commonly held notions of the world and opening to new perspectives. Our answers have not formed, but we are learning where to search. Given that the answers are so distant, the search itself must be fulfilling. To make progress, we must love the search itself, apart from the answers we find. Those of us determined to reach the end of this organizational search in our own lifetimes are doomed to frustration and false answers. Generations will pass before the answers become clear. And then, all of the searching likely will lead to discoveries of what was there all along. One of those discoveries will be that the organizational beasts we have alternately blessed and cursed are also the source of the fulfillment we seek. So, why not learn now to embrace them now, with all of their warts, wrinkles, and wonder. We must throw our arms around these crude creatures full of possibility.

What If the World Is Not Broken?

When we see the world in great disarray, it is easy to criticize what's wrong or what needs change. Admit it: Often we are saying, "What this world really needs is a dose of—*Me!*" But consider: You arrived here a few decades ago, delivered into a world that had already existed a few billion years prior to your transforming presence. Now . . . *You* know what's wrong? *You* are going to fix it? Billions of people before you used similar strategy in attempting to straighten the world's crooked ways. Others may not care or may be oblivious, but you care; you want to change things. But . . .

What if the world:

- is not broken?
- is not a chaotic mess at all, but we just don't understand it yet?
- is not crying out for us to impose our form of order?
- knows more about us than we do about it?
- has an order of its own?

What if to some larger mind, all that we are experiencing makes sense?

What if our real task is to find our place in what's been going on here for billions of years?

What if what we see as a "mess" is an invitation to discover ourselves?

This chapter has been about a chorus of questions, respecting and embracing the world as it is, whether in its raw and natural forms like thunderstorms or ocean tides, or its more adapted organizational forms like communities or committees. The world is not crying out for us to control it; many of us are crying out for something to control. The world—including the organizational world—has an order of its own, a "mind" of its own. Our opportunity and challenge is first to understand the world as it is, to wonder at it rather than to control it, to approach it with an awe, open to discovery. Wonder and awe are as useful to the realm of human organizations as to the rest of the natural realm. When we open ourselves to learning about the nature of the world, its organisms, and communities, we can see ourselves and our organizations with new eyes.

Chapter 3

Creating a Bureaucracy to Curse

The structures we live with today resulted from thousands of people before us seeking personal and organizational meaning and productivity. Our organizations were created by people as well intentioned and smart as ourselves, then we stepped into their creations. Whether we work for the schools, the military, a company, or a social agency, we stepped into quite similar structures based on related assumptions. Do some research at the next party you attend: Tell your favorite story about the bureaucracy's corrosive influence on important work. Will the people listening argue against the possibility of this happening? No. Will they wander off to seek more interesting conversation? No. They will stay because they know what you are talking about from their own experiences—and they want to tell you their favorite stories. Similar patterns of criticism occur in party after party, organization after organization, century after century. How might this centuries-old human pattern make sense? Why might we create organizations and then criticize our creations? We have repeated these patterns for generations; what can we learn from this?

We have a mental disconnect between our creation of bureaucracy and our use of it. We act as if we have nothing to do with the existence of the structures we love to curse, when in fact we assist in building them. This chapter is about four human predilections and their unintended consequences. People seek:

- achievement.
- predictability.
- stature.
- complexity.

Healthy individual actions lead to unhealthy organizations; understandable personal preferences lead to unfortunate organizational dynamics. It is our own daily choices that put us in our organizational dilemmas. Let's look at these four ways (among many) that we help tie our own hands.

Achievement

Huge, ineffective organizations have grown up over the centuries as a natural outgrowth of talented, invested people working together to do a good job. People do not set out to create these monsters, it just ends up that way. Actually, they set out to create work with meaning and direction. Then they get narrow and deep and bureaucratic because they are doing a good job and trying to do it better.

Years ago, C. Northcote Parkinson popularized attacks on bureaucracy with his little book, *Parkinson's Law.* The fact that he pointed out our foibles fifty years ago hasn't reduced our willingness to repeat history. He pointed to the British Navy after World War II, with twice the staff and half the fleet it had after World War I. But you and I don't have to look to the British Navy to find similar examples. Though it is convenient to single out staff functions guilty of this, the tendency to grow without regard for organizational limits has more to do with human nature than with some genetic defect peculiar to staff professionals.

We look for things to do that we can control. Having control over our work allows us to repeat it, to improve upon it, and to gain satisfaction from it. The control, the boundaries we establish, give us confidence about what is ours and allow us to predict that we will be able to do this again. We want to make a difference; we want to be important. Our need for significance is expressed through our work: When our work is important; we are important! Yes, it is a bit more complicated than that, but you get the idea.

And here comes the organization part, the building-the-bureaucratic-beast part:

- When I have important work in the organization, that work deserves the recognition and support and resources of the organization. I need more information, people, equipment, and money to bring this work to fruition.
- Or, I am attracted to those parts of the organization that have important work to do because I want to help; I want the significance that comes from being part of important work. So I gravitate in that direction.
- Or, my team has important work, which makes me important because they work for me. So I want their work to get recognition because that means I'm getting recognition: I'm important too!
- Or, I have routine work, but I don't have important work. So I will organize and routinize the work that I have. I will analyze and refine it; I will learn how to do it in the most time-efficient manner. This will help me and may be seen as significant by others.
- Or, I have my work, important or not, but it is *mine.* In order to do it well, without interference from others, I establish the boundaries of my work. And within the boundaries, I organize it the way I want it, making the outcomes more predictable to me.

Each alternative offers the possibility of accomplishment and significance, valued by myself and/or others. And each of these alternatives supports the growth of structure, initially within my job, then around my job, then within my job in relation to others, and so on until I have a bona fide organization. Allow that organization to function for a few months or years and it will settle into itself, locking in roles and relationships, systems and structures. What started out as searching, flexible, individual intentions turns into a concrete organizational structure.

No, it doesn't always work out that way, and yes, there are other elements not considered. But the larger point holds: We create the organizations we now curse, we do it out of understandable needs, and we don't know what we are creating as we are creating it. Our focus on what we are doing and what we want diverts us from the long-run implications of our acts. Work that passionately involves us is most seductive when we "know" the need to institutionalize our purpose and products.

Predictability

Much of what is written about organizations deals with order and control; it seems that's what organizations are for. Recent theories and models proclaim that if you use them, you will have more predictable success. That's appealing to organizations and individuals surrounded by uncertainty and buffeted by the marketplace. We all want to know how to repeat what we have done well before. In our search for security and certitude, we refine the structure of our work; we eliminate discovery, flow, and flexibility in favor of knowing. Freezing people and their actions in place becomes our way of knowing ahead of time what will happen. As their results become more predictable, they are often less productive.

The models, theories, and experts imply more predictability than they can deliver. The world often appears to have no order at all. Or if it does have an order, we cannot grasp it. In my experience, successful leaders respect the unpredictability of the world. Many of them delight in it. Leaders are not as linear and logical, as clear and coherent, as textbooks suggest. The same is true for other successful, happy people. Ask them why their lives work; their answers will vary. They are not paper cutouts of this or that life theory; they don't usually hold up a ten-step model and proclaim it as life.

Successful, happy people (and organizations) usually have a larger guidance in their lives, beyond any methodology or model. They reflect regularly on their meaning, intention, and purpose. They pay less attention to the roadmap and more attention to the needle of their compass. They are drawn toward their magnetic north, and they adjust to the terrain whether the map says there is a road there or not. None of this fits with order, control, and predictability. Yes, there is a place for structure, but it is at the boundary, not at the heart of fulfillment. Helping people point toward their own magnetic north is not as easy as installing a process or a model, asking everyone to learn and use it, and putting in some controls to make sure it's happening. Bureaucracy imposes order from the outside in, seeking performance that can only come from the inside out. There are no procedural substitutes for a person committed to a purpose.

The traditional organizational world aspires collectively to a perfection that we have never been able to realize individually. The organization wants to know that there will be no errors—and wants to know three months before the event. Predictability is prized. The organization depends on structure and process to eliminate doubt and the unforeseeable. We all participate in this as we try to show our knowledge and our power—and protect our jobs. In a pivotal organization meeting, you seldom hear someone exclaim, "That caught me completely by surprise!" In a bureaucracy, such a statement would be called "career-limiting." Surprises are visits (often gifts) from the world that exists outside of our plans.

Organizations help us resolve our life dilemmas. They put upon charts and into procedures the choices we are struggling with individually; they help us decide the answers—or they decide for us. They are biased in the direction of predictability so we will all know where we stand at the moment . . . and, for the purpose of coordination, where we will stand next. The question, "What shall I do next?" looks completely different to a middle manager in a large company and to a single mom at home with two kids. Their frameworks for answering the question, and the help they receive in answering the question, are completely different. What defines the difference is bureaucracy: The single mom creates her own order within her little organization—and without much help. The manager works within an organization that has previously considered what's needed and put structures in place to provide it. The home is filled with life, spontaneity, and chaos, while the office is filled with procedures, quiet, and order.

The security of knowing what is next is why many of us work in large organizations. We are there because of the regular work, the dependable resources, the interesting people, the fringe benefits, and the paychecks. We like being able to count on all of that. In return, we agree to do predictable things. We show up regularly and on time (in casual clothes on Friday); we do our work and follow the rules. We honor the culture, the rules, the roles of the organization. For many of us, this works for years and years, for a career. Others find this predictability stifling. We are torn between freedom/spontaneity and control/predictability. That part of us that opts for the predictable supports the growth of bureaucracy

Stature

Bureaucracy comes with hierarchy, and hierarchy tells us who is important—and not important—around here. Many of us who want to be important rely on hierarchy to confer stature upon us. In the military, rank and importance are displayed on sleeves, shoulders, or hats. In most of our organizations, the display is more subtle. It is who has the bigger desk, bigger cubicle, bigger plant, bigger budget, or bigger staff. Hierarchy is put in place to clarify responsibility and decision making, but has consequences going far beyond these controlling intentions.

Ego needs stature and hierarchy offers just that—or promises to with each move up a level. Hierarchy's consequences are myriad, and some are destructive. Those of us who would like to see ourselves as better than others are drawn to hierarchical ladders. When we are trying to win in the hierarchy game, we are inclined to focus more on what will elevate us and less on what's best for the larger organization. More levels and more people give us more opportunities in the hierarchy. All of this inclines those of us who are status seekers toward more bureaucracy.

If you were attending an important meeting, how would you react to being asked each of these questions: "What might you contribute?" "What level are you?"

The contribution question focuses on task, suggests working together, and implies that we are going to get something done and we hope you can be a part of it. It implies the need to learn; it is an honest inquiry and encourages more inquiry. The question about level says your importance is determined by where you are in the structure. It implies that you will receive attention appropriate to your level, not to what you bring. It leads to more and higher levels and functions. As we elevate ourselves, we complicate the organization.

Complexity

The fourth reason for creating organizations we love to curse complicates the first three. We simply do not recognize the impact of adding an individual, a level, or a function to an organization. We proceed in some innocence (because of many of the reasons cited earlier) taking small steps now that have profound implications later. Consider what happens to an organization of one as it expands to become six.

The simplest human organization is one individual. One person working by herself on a task:

- possesses all the skills available and knows who must do the job.
- processes information within herself; her thoughts and feelings do not need to be discussed in a meeting before being acted upon.
- decides intuitively without lengthy rationalizing and verbalizing.
- receives and integrates received information in her own way; she does not have to gain the agreement of others on how she will process information.

Work contained within one person is simple by comparison to our other options. This is not to argue that all work ought to be done by isolated individuals, but just to recognize the simplicity of this smallest, totally integrated organization. We seldom consider what is happening when we take the next step of moving beyond a person to a pair or a team. The initiating individual seldom says, "Actions like I'm about to take, create the bureaucracy I love to hate."

Move from a person to a pair of workers and complexity has increased greatly. Get beyond a pair to four, five, six people on a work team and there is a geometric increase in the complexity of working together. Yes, there are increases in the brain, muscle, or heart power available. Certainly, it can be worth the complicating consequences of adding workers, but recognize the simplicity of an individual working alone and the costs of more people working together. We seldom think of those costs when we are creating the organization. In a work team of six, each has a relationship with the other five; that's thirty relationships right there! Add the relationships between that team and others, complicating matters further. Maintaining those relationships requires telephone calls, meetings, memos, and e-mails; energy is expended, lost, and consumed, moving information, decisions, feelings, and tasks through a field of relationships. A department throws off a huge amount of heat and friction as people work across their roles, functions, and hierarchies. That energy burned is not available for other important work with customers, suppliers, other departments, or even family at home. Consider the many interactions, boundaries, partitions, and patterns around you. How much heat is generated internal to your group or function—energy not available for other uses?

People motivated to do good work that they can control will compound their own structure—very fertile ground for bureaucracy. As in . . .

- "We really could do this work better if we learned and everybody used this new software."
- "Georgia's work in human resources has been expanding. She wants to learn more about compensations systems. How about adding a generalist so she can focus more on compensation?"
- "According to our survey, a lot of people want this quarterly report on a monthly basis. That will take more time and staff, but the customer is asking for it."

These are not expressions of people trying to make work more complicated. These are the honest expressions of motivated individuals trying to help—and creating bureaucracy in the process. In discussions over coffee, they will wonder about how this place got so big and complicated, seeing no relationship to their own actions.

These interactions multiply to create organizations of some size. Corporations and agencies and governments are expanding to dimensions previously unknown. Members are more physically distant from the core purposes of the organization yet still a part of its purposes. Individuals are measured by quantified standards imposed from a distance. In the absence of a clear, compelling corporate purpose, people define their own. They "make up" the reasons they and their department exist. They talk about it among themselves. They create their own purpose, and boxes, the beginnings of their own little bureaucracy.

Your Choice

The four areas explored in this chapter—achievement, predictability, stature, and complexity—offer some explanation of why we create bureaucracy. Whatever the reasons, we create these bureaucracies over and over again, and we then criticize what we have created over and over again on some almost eternal wheel. We keep proclaiming this doesn't make sense—and we keep doing it! This forces me to a different conclusion: *Bureaucracy makes sense in ways we do not fully understand.* The four reasons for bureaucracy in this chapter are an attempt to say, "Yes, this makes sense!" Let's honor our experience rather than dismiss it. Let's affirm the bureaucracy we keep creating, not because we love it and want to enmesh ourselves in it, but because we cannot ignore the truth of our experience. Only then can we choose what we will do about organizations.

- We can resist them at every turn and do war with them.
- We can ignore them, hoping to disempower them by not giving them attention.
- We can attempt to understand them, to shape them into better servants of society.
- We can give up on them, despairing of the possibility of their doing anything constructive.
- We can create other choices.

There is also a cynical voice that deserves attention. We do not have to look or listen long before someone tells us how bad life is in this company or this church or this school or this city. People seem anxious to lament the hopelessness. At coffee breaks, coworkers elaborate on the unworkability of the system. Political leaders proclaim their disappointment in what's happening in Washington and try to bring us into their camp. Movies and television and comic strips draw cynical laughter from us in caricatures of organizations and executives. We, the hopeless people within organizations, then use all of this experience to reinforce ducking down, pulling back, and giving up. We even celebrate the failure of the organizations we work for; we congratulate ourselves on knowing better than to stick out our necks; we do what we can to fulfill our prophecy of organizational doom. The cynic sucks the breath out of organizations.

I have done much of this. Years ago, I met with four friends after work to have a beer and talk about the company we all worked for. This was an especially enlivened and competitive session: Five guys making fun of their bosses and other executives in the corporation. We were having a great time one-upping each other and generally demonstrating our superior knowledge about how this company ought to work—all at the expense of the leadership. Just before getting up to go home, and in a rare moment of authenticity, I said, "Hey, next time you guys get together to gripe at and make fun of the management, give me a call! This has been fun! On the other hand, if you want to get people together who are willing to do something constructive, count me out: I just gripe, I don't act." And I left.

Enough. I am tired of it. Tired of it in myself and in others. Tired of defining myself as a victim, as clever but weak, as incisive but inconsequential. That just does not fit with who I want to be; it does not fit with how I want to do my work, live my life interacting with organizations. Tired of lifting a half-empty glass to " . . . screwed-up organizations and all of us poor bastards suffering under them." Tired of toasting others' failures and weakness while celebrating my own superior knowledge and distance. Speaking the truth about myself to my four friends brought it home to me. I was at last aware of my complicity in bringing organizations down. When I realized that truth more deeply, I quit my patterned griping and looked for more opportunities to take part in helping organizations succeed. I began to breathe life into, rather than suck life out of, organizations.

Coming to Terms With Bureaucracy

In our search for conspirators working to entrap us in this bureaucracy, we shine our lights on . . . a huge mirror. We discover that we are busily creating these organizations that we then rail against. We pursue achievement, predictability, stature, and complexity for ourselves with little thought to our impact on the future of the organization. What we conceive has consequences far beyond what we intended. We are the parents of this beast—and the children of it. It reflects no better purpose than what we bring; it offers no more hope than we hold; it inspires no better life than we give.

Come to terms. Come to terms with what you love and hate about these bureaucratic creatures. Come to terms with what they give to you and take from you. Consider the deal you've made with these devils and angels in your life. You have been defining the deal for years; now, step back and see your patterns. Honestly, what have you been doing? Use this model to help in that consideration:

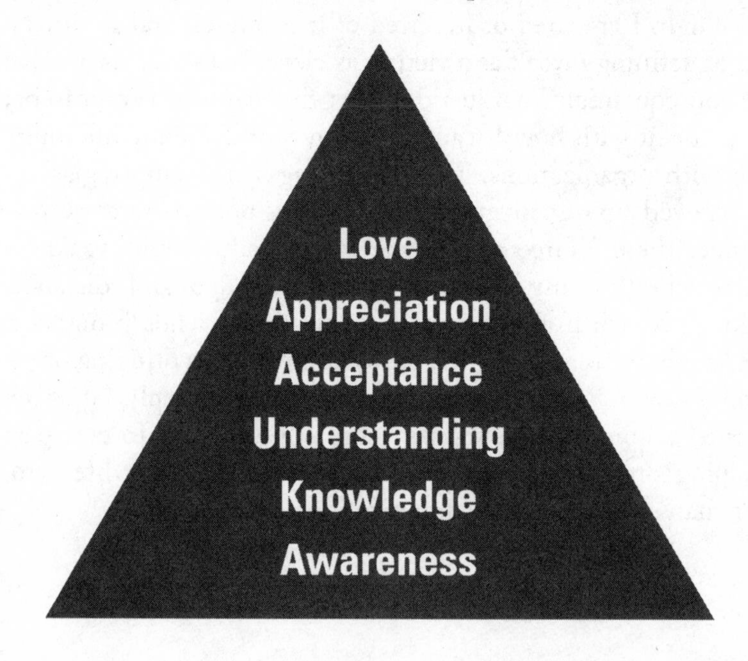

First a few words about this model as it might apply outside organizations. With an old friend in mind, recall those elements of your friendship that fit with the phases of this model. Recall your initial awareness of the person. Remember getting to know more about him or her. Think about reaching some deeper understanding of who that person is. Remember moments when you felt full acceptance of your friend—your friend's thoughts, feelings, life choices. Think about times when you appreciated that person for who he or she was—his or her uniqueness. Recall times when you felt especially loving toward your friend. These six phases are expressed much more distinctly in this model than they exist in real life; I'm oversimplifying your friendship to help you see six aspects of it.

Let's apply those same six phases to your developing relationship with an organization. With one organization in mind—perhaps your employer or a client—answer these questions, using the six-phase model as your starting point:

- Describe your relationship with this organization as it has developed so far, beginning with awareness and moving toward love.
- Select and explain two phases that best represent the relationship now.
- What encourages you most about the relationship to this point?
- What do you struggle with most in deepening your relationship with this organization?
- What might the future hold for this relationship?
- Who are the key people that your relationship focuses upon within the organization?
- What could you do with those key people to help them look at the relationship with you?

These questions and their answers carry you further along the path with this organization and the people in it. Your ease, or disease, with it affects everything that happens. If you are angry or not accepting of the organization, that will show through. If you are dependent, that determines your reactions. If you have a deep appreciation, that colors all you do. Wherever you are in the six phases, whatever your stance toward this organization, has consequences. Step back, look, and see what you are creating.

Simply said, the key to embracing the beast of bureaucracy is the higher three phases of this model: acceptance, appreciation, and love. Most of us do much better on the three lower phases: becoming aware, knowledgeable, and understanding. We often create gaps at just the point we should be closing them; we step back at the point we should step forward. We worry that fully embracing the current organization requires continuing in that same mode. Not true—no more than you have to take up all the characteristics and habits of a dear friend. In fact, you can detest some of the actions your friend has taken and also embrace the friend for the effort he or she has made. The same is true for organizations.

We finish Part One, having explored the good reasons bureaucracy comes into being and our likely complicity in all of that. We also have a better understanding of how our stance toward organizations—our loving or hating—affects all that we do within them. Together, we are the life of our organizations: As we breathe, so they breathe. What we choose, they become.

Part Two

Searching for the Beauty

"What a beauty to behold!" How often do we hear that phrase applied to an organization? To a person, a beach, a film, an automobile, a flower, a symphony, a soccer match, or a sunset maybe, but to an organization? Though each of us appreciates what is beautiful in our lives, we often think of it as something that happens outside of our work. The next three chapters are about discovering the beauty in the organizations around us; helping our senses pick up the shapes, sounds, scents, colors, movement, and tastes that we comb through in search of the beautiful. Those senses don't automatically shut down when we go to work, but many of us shut them down. When we do not expect to find beauty at work, we are less likely to find it. And of course, in many organizations there isn't much there. In the fairy tale, Belle had to look long and hard to find the beauty she hoped the Beast held. She was rewarded; we may or may not be.

But beautiful organizations are possible too. In fact, you likely have seen a few in operation: when a family does a particularly good job of piling everything in the car for a week's vacation; or when a work team spins off into a highly creative session; or when the school Parent Teachers Association cooperates to bring new learning to the classroom. There are millions of small examples like these that express or hint at beauty and its larger possibilities in an organization.

In our companies and agencies, departments and divisions, we need to know what beauty is if we are to see it or create it. We need ideals to compare with our experience—just like in any other realm where beauty is valued. And that is what this part of the book is about: our ideals and aspirations for organizations. When we can imagine or know what we want, we will more likely be able to find it or create it. Imagining and knowing comes before creating the beautiful organizations we would like to experience more often. Through these chapters, we will gain glimpses of beauty now present in the organizations we serve. Imagining beautiful future organizations is not normally an executive pastime, and discovering the beauty already present is a challenge to most of today's organizations.

There must be beauty within this beast; the present organization must hold within itself the potential to be seen as beautiful by many people. If there is nothing there to please the eye, the mind, the heart of anyone, the organization lacks the healthy essence needed to thrive for the benefit of itself, its members, and the world around it. Others may choose to support it, but you do not have to. You can choose to leave, to take your search for life somewhere else. Part Two will help you consider what you want from organizations, what potential you are fulfilling. It will help you put your aspirations for organizations beside the realities you faced in the first part of this book. This is the most reflective part of the book; it asks you to think deeply and not take any action . . . yet. Be patient with yourself and what these chapters ask of you; it's groundwork for the commitment you need to renew organizations.

Some Stimulating Assumptions

How do we rethink what organizations are about? What can we do to make it more likely we will step outside the boundaries defined by our long experience with these huge creatures? A good place to start is by challenging our reinforced experience and perspective, by questioning our implicit assumptions built from years in traditional organizations. In fact, more than questioning them, replacing them. We are more likely to reach a new place when we start off with different assumptions; we are more likely to end up someplace we are unaccustomed to, and that is at least movement, if not progress.

I decided to look at organizations using some assumptions that feed the richness of human life. Bear with me on these; you may find yourself supporting these assumptions or questioning them. That matters less than striking out in a new direction. I have chosen one; you could chose another. That said, here are some assumptions that, when acted on, feed a healthy human life:

- Intentional actions do not yield predictable, understandable results. We do not know how much difference we are making with anything we do. Any measures we attempt, though useful, focus on a shallow and narrow portion of what difference we make. This assumption allows us to respect the natural chaos (or larger, as yet unknown order) that surrounds us, rather than act as if we are in control of everything.
- Pursuing new learning is in itself valuable even when the destination is unclear—perhaps especially when the destination is unclear. Learning is partly a process of discovering what is happening anyway, and then following it. This assumption values the process of learning more than its outcomes.

- We are reaching for and contributing to outcomes we will never see. We are like laborers on a medieval cathedral: We do our work, we imagine what we are building, yet we never see the work completed. It is work worth doing—and hopefully our great-great-great-grandchildren will be present and proud at the dedication. Our important work joins the work of others over generations of generations—whether we are aware of it or not . This assumption moves us beyond the timeframe of our lives and away from the egocentric implication that everything worth our work will happen in our lifetime.

These assumptions are at odds with the organizational traditions most of us have grown up within. They do not attempt to secure the predictability and control that defines so much of what organizations are about. They don't seek security; they presume less and leave much more for us to discover. Perhaps they lead toward too little of the structure we need for organizations to work. Or maybe they will stimulate some new ideas that will help revitalize organizations.

Past and Present and Possibility

We often assume that if we know an organization's Past, that will help us understand its Present, and that will point us toward its Future. Many of us grew up within that logical, linear sense and are not finding it all that useful. Too often, it just does not work. We need new assumptions that lead us to a Future with more organizational possibilities; that's what our earlier list was doing. Let's extend that list of assumptions with five related to time:

- We are creating the Future now whether we are aware of it or not. The Future is happening regardless of what we do about it. Our challenge is to become aware of our role in creating the Future. We can impact the Future *now,* rather than waiting to see what will happen to us later.

- The Future is not projected from the Past and through the Present; it is not simply an extension of what we already know.
- Immersion in the Present and Past keeps us from clarifying the Future we aspire to. We cannot see the wide array of Future possibilities while wrapped up in today. We must temporarily step out of today's frameworks and assumptions to get a glimpse of tomorrow's possibilities.
- Clarity about our Future aspirations allows us to see the Present and Past in a new way, with new opportunities. When we hold on to these Future aspirations, they influence our every action. We imagine where we want to go, and then use that imagined destination to guide us in what we do now. We can be guided as much by what we want as by what we know.
- Implementing our Future aspirations requires appreciating the Past and Present, while making their connection to the Future visible and tangible to others.

Though we separate Past, Present, and Future, they are connected, dependent on each other. Building walls between them distorts the reality of their overlap, their simultaneity. When we deal with one, we are dealing with the other two; we cannot really choose to deal with them separately. Renewing an organization requires clear aspirations informing Past, Present, and Future. Renewing requires breathing life into the organization *now*. The next three chapters build from these assumptions.

Chapter 4

Essential Questions for Organizations

We spend our days immersed in the people, processes, and products of organizations. No avoiding this and no reason to, but there is more to organizations than results, end points, and outputs. There is their beginning, their conception, their genetic code, their essence. That's what we will pursue here. Organizations may live within the limits of the "genetic coding" they were born with; they may have this built-in limitation, if we are assuming they share our own mortality. What if we were to look at them more expectantly? What if we were to assume the possibility of very long life? This chapter engages in the search for the organizational "fountain of youth." If we know what long life is about, then we can attempt to create conditions under which it might flourish.

What is so great about long-lived organizations? If more organizations included within their purpose their intent to live hundreds of years, they would behave quite differently. Too many of today's corporations live for the next financial quarter's results. Imagine the set of questions confronting an organization that wants to make it through the next financial period, versus those considered by a company that has been here 200 years and wants to be here at least 200 more. I'm imputing good to those organizations with the longer vision, the longer aspiration. It provides a strong counter to the short-term selfishness we so often experience.

We Are Living Our Questions

"How can I find happiness?" This familiar question provokes many of the actions most of us take each day. Happiness now . . . and now . . . and now. Unending happiness is not available to me in this life, but that does not stop me from asking how I might achieve it. And it's unattainability does not keep me from wanting it and working toward it. Ambitious questions with unattainable answers are the ones truly worth pursuing. They stretch us; they take us to our outer boundaries and help us reach beyond.

We are defined by our questions more than our answers. Ask me what I have done and you will hear my history; ask me what I aspire to and you will hear my dreams and longings. Consider the questions that recur in your life; consider the answers you seek. Here are intriguing, unanswerable questions that many of us keep asking:

- Who am I?
- Who am I becoming?
- What gives my life meaning?
- What give my work meaning?
- What am I doing here?
- How can I live a long, full life?
- How can I find happiness?

You probably have recycled some of these questions many times. The fact that you have asked the same question before does not keep you from asking it again. You likely have a few questions that you return to regularly and with each visit come to deeper appreciation of the question's depth, its mystery, its intrigue—if not its answer. The compelling questions draw you on and define your purpose. You are pulled toward the unknown; you are drawn forward without a clear destination; you are searching for deeper meaning in your life. Even when you are not aware of the search, you are on the search.

Those large, living creatures we call organizations have questions too—questions voiced, questions implicit in their actions, questions that draw them toward their destiny. Some are immediate questions like, "How do we increase this quarter's return on investment?" Some are strategic questions like, "How do we achieve economies of scale?" Some are market-oriented questions like, "How do we stay competitive?" Any question can become defining for the moment. Like us, these organizations are defined by their questions more than by their answers. Here are a few questions you may have heard through your work:

- What is our purpose?
- What will we look like twenty years from now?
- What is our core competence?
- What difference do we make in the marketplace? In the community? In the world?
- What will be the next development in our field? How might we get there?
- What can we do to assure our continued existence?

Notice the parallels between these questions and those posed of the individual earlier. Notice the reach of the questions, the draw to the unknown future. These too are questions returned to again and again, questions that pull the organization toward an intriguing and unknown future. And the beauty of the organization is revealed in the pursuit. To the extent that the organization honors the pursuit of its larger questions, it is creating its future. Its aspirations for the future become the lens through which today is seen; today's actions incline it toward an imagined tomorrow.

Reframing the World With Our Questions

How might we think beyond the restraints that come with today's organizations? How do we get over the immediacy, the time compression, the growing stack of priorities, to imagine an organization that serves everyone invested in it—shareholders, citizens, workers, communities, customers, allies—and the world itself? We do it by reconsidering our assumptions about its life and life span.

As things stand now, organizations come into being, live, and die. Along the way, they go through various life stages that might be compared to a person moving from childhood through adolescence to adulthood and eventually death. They will likely merge or restructure or reshape themselves significantly many times during their life. Look in on the organization at any time and you will probably find its members engaged in the compelling issues of the moment, working hard to keep up with what is assailing them from all sides. Their heads are down, they are working furiously to resolve this problem so they can move on to the next . . . and they have been doing this for years. They are focused on surviving now. Step into any organization and ask the leadership, "Why do you keep doing this?" and you will likely see confused expressions reflecting a combination of recognition, impatience, and a need to get back to work. We do not have time for these questions—even when we have a glimmer of their importance.

And don't we know the parallel situations in our own lives? Swimming hard, usually keeping our heads above water, approaching our limits, and occasionally hearing, "Why do you keep doing this?" It's difficult to think about this question while swimming, and swim we must, so we put it aside—not without some gnawing knowledge that we are avoiding what is important in favor of what is urgent. Our situation is quite parallel to that of organizations. What usually happens to change things for us or for other individuals? One answer is: not much. We continue to swim until we die; we live with this nagging problem and it continues to drag on us. But there are better responses than that. What about those who do confront it? How does that happen?

For some reason, we step out of the world as we have framed it; we begin to see the world differently. Usually something or someone gets our attention. One common reason for altering our perspective is tragedy. Our doctor warns us that our life is at risk. Or our spouse threatens to leave. Or a neglected child makes desperate cries for attention. Or our heart rebels at the demands on it. Or a loved one dies. It is not always tragedy that reminds and shifts us to a larger perspective; some of us are strong and wise enough to shift ourselves. But whatever way it happens, we say, "This is not working. . . . There must be more to life than this. . . . I wonder what it is. . . . I am going to find a larger life for myself." We redefine what is meaningful in our lives; we renew our purpose; we act accordingly. And our new meaning and purpose often leads us to aspire to live less for self and more for others, to contribute to a larger community, to the fuller expression of our own humanity, to greater respect and love for the people around us. We commit to more transcendent values and purpose that will still have life long after we are dead. We do all of this by stepping back from immediate engagement with the world. We move to a lofty height where we see and reflect on our whole life and beyond. From this vantage, we decide what is important and what we will do about it.

Imagine an organization going through a parallel process. Imagine it stepping back from the pursuit of profit, or funding, or position—whatever drives it now—and saying, "This is not working. . . . There must be more to life than this. . . . We wonder what it is. . . . We are going to find that larger life for ourselves." Individuals turn in this direction and organizations must too—if they are to have a purpose beyond running after today's profits and priorities.

- ✧ How can our organization thrive now while honoring the ideals it upholds?
- ✧ What must live beyond this organizational generation? What are we doing about that?
- ✧ How do today's plans reflect our larger purposes and values?
- ✧ How can we help people succeed now, recognizing they are here for a short time in the life of the organization?
- ✧ What is necessary for our organization to exist for centuries?

These questions pursue the essence of organizational longevity—what lives beyond the life of any one individual, system, division, product, term of office, administration, service, or structure. The questions reach for the unattainable, knowing that to reach is more fulfilling than to grasp.

Of course, some organizations live short, yet useful lives. Short-term existence and purpose are legitimate too; not everyone and everything needs to live with a sense of permanence. Just because an organization is vital now does not mean it should be here forever. Our bodies don't live forever and organizations don't have to either. Headlines about restructuring, hiring, firing, layoffs, delayering, and relocations testify to the organic nature of organizations as they seek to sustain their lives with different facilities, systems, settings, markets, and people. I'm not suggesting that all organizations do this expanding and contracting sensitively; but there is no built-in requirement for them to continue to hold a certain form, provide a certain product, or employ certain people. And there is no requirement that they work within the framework of the questions offered on the previous page.

There are also organizations that care nothing about the above questions, but rather care only about the bottom line now. And there are well-intentioned organizations that have no time for this attempt at transcendent thinking, who see no relationship between what they are doing and the condition of the world. And there are selfish, short-sighted, greedy organizations and people that would close this book on these paragraphs. My questions are for all of them, for all of us, whether we are now seriously asking the questions or not. These questions are for the part of the organization, and the part of you, that longs for organizations to make a finer contribution to the world.

Many organizations do think about the future beyond today. They examine their aspirations, they ponder their legacy—and see themselves coming up short. Disheartened, they see themselves falling into the gap between what they really should be (if they were any good) and their present (rather sorry) state. Other organizations see in the same situation the immersion in a swirl of forces calling out for constant, innovative adaptation, ripe for influence in the pursuit of their aspirations. There may be thousands of people in dozens of locations greatly complicating this pursuit of opportunity, but *underneath it all there is an organism choosing to define itself.* Individuals and organizations are free to find their own perspective: Fall into the gap or live lives in the creative swirl.

Every action an individual or an organization takes does not have to be fraught with profound implications. We can still fritter away an evening sitting in front of the TV or puttering around the house. An organization can waste resources impressing a visiting executive, or building detailed plans and procedures that will never be used. The occasional "lapse" into lethargy or self-importance or fussing with details does not have to be condemned; it's the patterns that are important.

Life

Life is first of the two core values essential to organizational success that continues for generations. Ascendance is the second core value, and we will consider it shortly. Life is *the capacity for growing in the present.* All hope for continued life is centered on the capability of supporting growth now. A life-centered organization is dedicated to seeing that life today feeds life for generations to come. This core value informs every decision; it is more important than any one product or service or part of the organization. Everyone within this organization knows it must have the continuing capacity to feed itself, to thrive. Organizations that want to survive for generations must have life now, but they must have more than just the ability to stay alive at this moment. An organization must be a reliably fertile ground, a place where life is constantly created, nourished, supported. It must be a place where the sources of life are replenished as well, a place where life can take root again and again. Read this paragraph again, converting "organization" to "individual" for a richer sense of the meaning of life.

Think about one organization you know well and consider these questions:

- ✧ How is "life" defined in this organization?
- ✧ What creates life for this organization? For members?
- ✧ What will renew the life of this organization indefinitely?
- ✧ How are other lives nourished by what this organization does? Stakeholders? Communities? Society? The world?
- ✧ What is this organization doing to ensure its life for generations?
- ✧ How does this organization contribute to the long-term survival of itself, its people, its communities, and the planet?

This is not a save-the-world view; it's a we-are-creating-ourselves-and-the-world view. This is not a call to action; it's recognizing the impact of the actions the organization is already taking on the long-term nourishment or starvation of itself, its communities, and its planet. Every organization is busily demonstrating its own answers to the above questions. Watch long enough and you will see the implicit answers. Consider nearly the same questions with a small organization like the family in mind:

- How is life defined in this family?
- What creates life for this family? For members?
- What will renew the life of this family indefinitely?
- What does this family aspire to pass on, generation to generation?
- How are other lives nourished by what this family does? Friends? Neighbors? Community? Society? The world?
- How does this family help people and the planet survive indefinitely?

In this life-filled perspective, the questions apply at all levels from individual to the family to the corporation, to the government and to the globe. Attending to life means being conscious of answers to questions like these. The opportunity for the corporate organization is to enhance the lives of employees, customers, the marketplace, and the world. The opportunity for the civic organization is to enhance life for its citizens, for the community, and for society as a whole. Most of what we now practice about enhancing life starts with ourselves and is confined to those immediately around us, in a limited time frame. We need to widen our reach.

Ascendance

Now to the second core value, ascendance. Ascendance means *rising toward future completeness.* The word "ascend" is familiar to us; we hear it and think of "rising" or "climbing"; both meanings fit with my notion of ascendance. Combine "ascend" with "essence" and you are closer to the meaning I am seeking: something that of its nature lifts toward its perfection.

Ascendance is an unfamiliar, intriguing word. Put it beside "organization" and you get an "ascendant organization." That conjures up shapes and energies I do not usually associate with organizations. For example, an ascendant organization would have an ingrained tendency to rise, to reach toward its future fullness, to long for its more complete and perfect state. This inclination would be so much of its nature that the organization could not long be diverted from pursuit of this purpose; it would turn toward it again and again. The organization would know and feel the pull toward this potential, a potential always over the horizon and never fully realized. Everything now present would be in service to this wonderful, elusive, and distant future state. The organization today would excel because it is drawn toward its own perfection. Questions like these would help an organization in the discovery of its ascendance:

- What is this organization rising toward?
- What impact does this rising toward completeness have on people and communities around it?
- What will this organization put in place that will allow future organizational generations to ascend?
- What will we be proud to pass on to the next generation?
- How can we incorporate these aspirations into every moment of organizational life?

These questions can be asked of an individual or a family or a nation. I recall these questions coming up in my work and personal life. For example, I recall sitting in on a meeting with a group of older hourly workers, most of whom had invested their entire work life in this one manufacturing plant. They were close to retirement and talking about what they hoped they were passing on to the generations of workers that would follow them. I'm also recalling conversations with my parents about their hopes and dreams for us, their children. Both conversations fit with these questions and my notions of ascendance.

From the family organization perspective, we usually think of ourselves as "descendants," coming from those who lived before us. That conventional expression is a perspective reflecting children's subordination to past generations, emphasizing where we came from. Putting my notion to work, children could be considered "ascendants" rather than descendants. See the difference?

Future-focused . . . reaching toward completeness . . . building from the generations that came before . . . creating a world for future ascendants. Imagine your children as ascendants . . . and imagine ascendant cultures . . . and ascendant agencies . . . and companies and communities and societies.

An Ascendant Life

Life: The capacity for growing in the present.
Ascendance: Rising toward future completeness.

Life and ascendance cannot do it alone, but they are seed ingredients. The meanings of ascendance and life combine in the phrase, "the ascendant life"; each word informs and deepens the other. An ascendant life becomes something you might aspire to, whether you are an individual, a family, a company, or a town by asking these questions:

- Does this organization have the capacity to rise and grow for generations toward its own completeness?
- What would an ascendant life mean for it?
- What might it be ascending toward?
- How do our views of the present state of the organization change with an ascendant life perspective?

These questions expand consideration beyond the calls of daily life. My continued emphasis on the need for this ascendant, focus-on-creating-the-future perspective does not mean you or your organization will get there. It's not because it is attainable that we are drawn toward this future state; in fact we are drawn there because we *cannot* capture it in our lifetimes—a concept consistent with the early assumptions we are building upon. That mysterious and alluring future draws us forward and in the process suggests what we might do differently today; it creates a healthy restlessness. Our dedication to creating something more than what we inherited offers the possibility of expansive human thought and action right now, right here, on the ground, in this organization, today. The resolution of our most intractable organizational issues comes not from a head-on dealing with the problems or attempting to escape them, but from redefining it with this new perspective and in new terms. That is ascendant life at work.

Chapter 5

Aspiring to Life

My search for life in organizations comes from years of working with people engaged, willingly or not, in change. Those seeing the need for change—regardless of their assigned role—see themselves as leaders, revolutionaries, bureaucrats, missionaries, the disenfranchised, the threatened, the empowered, the weak, or the chosen. When I listen to this chorus of voices, I hear a refrain. See if you can hear it as they sing out their many questions. The song begins with, How do we create organizations that:

- yield a high return for what we are investing—all the time, money, material, mind, muscle, emotion, spirit, and energy?
- sustain themselves through time and regenerate themselves through time?
- contribute to the vitality of members and the surrounding community?
- are self-aware, self-directing, self-moderating, and self-reflecting?

- encourage members to become their better selves?
- encourage other organizations to become their better selves?
- respect the entire lives of people and organizations—physical, mental, emotional, and spiritual?
- engage others in creating the purpose this organization is rising to?
- recognize the value of life beyond this organization?
- contribute to the world?

Visit any organization and you can hear the refrain. People are crying out their need to be different or better or more. They may be singing lamentations of pain from what they lack, or their songs may be celebrations of what they have. In any case, they have a sense of what is possible beyond what they now know; they yearn for that better place and they are drawn to creating it for themselves and for those who follow them. The refrain emerges from the singing of all the verses, all of the questions. Together they reveal the melody.

This chapter writes an answering song, one which feeds the need people are singing out for—like a love duet in an opera or musical in which passionately sung longings are matched with equally passionate promises of fulfillment, creating organizations that are:

- a joy to work in.
- celebrated by the communities they serve.
- filled with daily reminders of higher values and purpose.
- experienced as a "lifting tide" by everyone who works there.
- committed to enhancing the lives of everyone touched by their product or service.
- places where everyone would love to have their children work.
- appreciated by owners as much more than just a good investment.

- receptive to ideas coming from the communities around them.
- dedicated to living for generations.

Imagine working in an organization that holds up these outcomes as its fulfillment. Because of its choices, it would be viewed by people as a valued contributor, a good citizen, a worthy employer, and a good investment for years and years. That organization would have celebrations and scrapbooks and web sites full of testimony, headlines and awards—external recognition testifying to its internal accomplishments. This is not to say that every customer and stockholder would be attracted to it, but it would be demonstrating what many are seeking.

If those are outcomes many of us are seeking, what might lead us there? I return to the answers offered in the previous chapter, Life and Ascendance. But it is a long path from discovering these answers to becoming an organization as fulfilled and fulfilling as we might imagine. The distance may be daunting, but the destination is compelling for those of us seeking higher organizational purpose and meaning.

Daily, immediate, and pragmatic reasons turn us away from ascendant opportunities. The priority is often short-term objectives that could be jeopardized, or there is no profit, or you don't get the credit; or the rewards are so distant and unlikely, or you don't know how to make this leap—all reasons to put aside your organizational dreams and keep doing what you have been doing. Go ahead; put them aside, but consider the consequences of this accommodation. Slouch back into familiar roles, doing what you have done for years to get recognition and money, dropping hope for anything more; leave the pursuit of higher goals to social agencies and churches. Find your reinforcement for this among coworkers also opting to play the old game. You will be making a legitimate choice—and in the midst of this, you will hunger for more.

Aspirations for Ascendant Organizations

Aspirations focus on aspects of the distant future an organization is drawn to creating. Aspirations provide an organizational morality, something that is "right," that the organization both reaches for and judges itself against. Aspirations are far beyond the products and services of the moment; they even supersede the type of business or agency or institution as it now exists. An aspiration serves not only the organization and its members, but the world; it embodies a spirit of participation in the success of the world around it rather than an isolation and greediness.

What might an organization aspire to in its reach toward ascendance and life? I will offer eight aspirations as answers to that question. Each of my aspirations points toward ascendance and life; each leans toward organizational completeness; each suggests action. Together they paint a picture of what I am reaching for. But my eight aspirations may not be yours. Use my list as the starting point for developing your own.

These eight aspirations are expressed from two perspectives: those of the individual member and of the combination of all individuals who form the organization. To return to the music metaphors used earlier, if the individual is the soloist, the organization is the choir. The individual's aspirations have a strength of their own, and blend to give voice and life to organization. Together, individuals create an organization that has a life of its own, both separate from and dependent on the people who formed it. Listen to the soloist and the choir, the individual and the organization in these aspirations.

Purpose

Individual: Work is an essential way I pursue my life meaning. I aspire to my better self, my completeness, my purpose through my work. I work in an organization that will live far into the future, providing future generations the opportunity for livelihood and fulfillment—as it has supported me and the people here before me.

Organization: Our purpose is our pursuit of what we aspire to become. We are drawn into the future through commitment to this purpose. Our purpose is advanced when people understand our intentions, our plans, our possibilities, and how they might participate. Explicit in all of this is our intent to survive and contribute for generations. Everything supports purpose—products, services, structure, systems, strategy, roles, members.

Worth

Individual: My sense of self-worth is enhanced by working here. My work is valued; I am valued. I work in surroundings and with people who respect what I bring and make good use of me. I take pride and satisfaction in doing worthwhile work.

Organization: We are acclaimed for the unique, substantive products and services we offer to the world and its inhabitants. We intend to create products and services that have a long and useful life. We want whatever we do to be valuable to consumers and to be recognized for the value it adds.

Stewardship

Individual: I am invested in making good use of the resources at my disposal. I feel responsible for the materials, information, people, equipment, money, and natural resources I work with. This responsibility comes with doing a good job and being a good citizen.

Organization: We are a model for other organizations in our stewardship of resources, be they financial, human, material, or natural. We see use of resources as the privilege accompanying our purpose, rather than a burden or a right. We know we earn this privilege, and that we make a difference in the world through how we exercise it.

Contribution

Individual: Through my work and the results of my work I see that I make a positive difference; I am a contributor. What I do goes beyond the work itself to the work environment and the lives of people I work with—and beyond to others who use what I produce.

Organization: We consciously and systematically ask what special contributions we might make to the marketplace and the world. We aspire to offer unique products and services with widespread benefits, not disproportionately accruing to some while neglecting others. We are contributing to an overall sense of global health and well-being. We intend to be generous in what we contribute and are seen as such. We want this world to be more full of life because of our presence.

(Before continuing, imagine possible uses for the four aspirations expressed so far. Eventually this high-flying thinking has to be brought down to the ground of daily reality. Consider the effect of these aspirations on plans, questions, discussions, analysis, commitment, and action. Imagine how an individual or a work team, or how you might use these aspirations. Take a minute to reinforce the practical side of this lofty list before moving on.)

Identity

Individual: Work provides opportunities for my personal discovery and expression. Work helps identify who I am by what I do. The workplace recognizes that I am more than just "a worker" but "a person who works." I have also learned about the talents and perspective that other people bring to work; I like the experience of working with unique individuals.

Organization: We define ourselves as a strong, individual organization. We help everyone inside and outside the organization to understand our present boundaries—what we are and are not. Our unique identity is important. Being clear about it enables us to work better with others different from us. We value their individuality as we value our own.

Interdependence

Individual: I expect to rely on others I work with both inside and outside the organization. I know that together we have the potential to do much more than we could do individually. I am willing to do the hard work of forming and maintaining a team because of the unique experience and results possible. My work also holds the potential for friendships that build from what we have done together.

Organization: We know and love the fact that our success is dependent on others. As much as we value our individuality, we know our life depends on many, many partnerships with other people and organizations in the world. We search for partners in our endeavors; we encourage a wide range of human interaction consistent with our purpose. We want to meet people's social needs as a part of their work. We expect and hope people will grow to care for each other as they depend on each other.

Community

Individual: My communities are essential to my life. In all that I do, I am a part of them. I value and feel valued by the communities I participate in—work, customer, civic, trade, and professional. I search out and identify with various communities of people joined in common purpose. I see them as vital to my learning, productivity, perspective, contribution, and identity. Our organization recognizes the importance of these communities.

Organization: We are active participants in the various communities in which we reside and serve. We strive to do our part to support the success of these communities; we know they are the source of our life. We encourage the growth of communities within our organization. They have become the primary locus for building the talent, motivation, and accomplishment the organization needs. Our systems and structures are set up to respect these internal communities, involving them in the larger organization.

Hope

Individual: My work and workplace encourages me to expect the best of the future. I am inclined to see the possibilities in whatever comes my way at work. I know I can influence what is happening and I look for opportunities to do so. The future is important to what I do in the present.

Organization: We deal in a marketplace larger than money; we see a world full of opportunity—opportunity for us to pursue our purpose, to bring our aspirations to reality. We feel our responsibility to help create a world in which everyone sees positive possibilities in their future. We encourage others we work with to mirror our hopefulness, to avoid slipping into despair as a pattern of dealing with the world. We hold out great hopes, hopes that reach far beyond what can be accomplished in any one human lifetime—and all the more worth reaching for because of that.

These eight aspirations, rooted in the desire to create an organization that lasts for generations, uphold the importance of long life; all else is subordinate. These aspirations proclaim that today's greatest accomplishments matter because they support this organization's longevity. No product or service is sacred; no market or structure is untouchable. These eight aspirations infuse the organization with life; they don't just create systems or strategies, services or structures. The organization's products are byproducts of the aspirations. The main "product" is continued life of the organization itself. Everything is considered in relation to what gives this organization capacity for growing in the present and rising toward its future completeness. When we bring this down to one question, it is, *"Does this serve Life?"*

My eight aspirations may have elicited a few of your own, aspirations different from mine, hopefully in harmony with mine, but not necessarily. Note what you aspire to. What are you trying to create that might serve the world well now, and generations from now? What would you like to remind yourself of each day when you are in the middle of sorting out your work and life? Aspirations require a reach, and must be worth reaching for regularly, in the present, not just in the middle of a book. Returning to them consistently in the work setting changes that setting and the dynamics within it. That is the challenge: to embody, to *in-corp*orate, them in the corporation, to make them part of the body of the organization. And how might we do that? You may have come up with some examples; here are some of mine:

- ✧ Develop a list for your own organization, whatever it might be—yourself, your work team, your PTA. Ask yourselves, "What is it that we are reaching for together, that would result in the continued life of this organization, and would draw us toward greater fulfillment?"
- ✧ Read or ask about organizations that have lived for hundreds of years through a vast array of political, social, and economic changes. What positive forces seemed to be at work in those organizations that allowed them to last through the centuries?
- ✧ Imagine that tomorrow you will be speaking with your children or grandchildren or a class at a local school, telling them a few aspirations that have guided your life that you think could serve them well too. What would you tell them?
- ✧ Read through your organization's literature searching for the implicit underlying aspirations that have guided it thus far. What is it that leader after leader, strategy after strategy, policy after policy, through good times and bad, has held forth for the customers? For the workers? For the communities? For the shareholders? For the world?

The Rewards

What might happen when we get intentional about our aspirations—personal and organizational? The rewards are different from the satisfaction of beating a deadline or satisfying a customer or pleasing your boss or finishing a project. When pursuing aspirations that will never be fully realized, we need some immediate rewards for progress we make. Consider the quality of the following rewards for you, the individual—and think about their organizational counterparts:

- Your world becomes larger; there are more paths than you earlier imagined.
- Your source of rewards is internal—and more under your control.
- You have less panic when something goes wrong today.
- Your sense of urgency is reduced; you are more patient.
- You shift from blaming toward acceptance and forgiveness.
- You apply yourself where you can be influential.
- You are more intent on learning from all that surrounds you.
- You are less attached to results while maintaining your investment in action.
- You notice your progress in reaching toward fuller expression of yourself.
- Your clarity about who you are gives you more control over your life.

Chapter 6

Signs of Life in Your Organization

As critical as I am of organizations, I see them as a daunting, yet inevitable opportunity: We are not going to create a productive, interdependent world without them. Many seem determined to block the accomplishments they proclaim they want; the human reach toward happiness and potential is constantly challenged by them; and the health of the planet and its occupants is profoundly affected by what they do. And "they," after all, are made up of "us."

There are encouraging signs of life in organizations and we will identify some of them here. We will not attribute perfection to any organization, but instead take encouragement from what we can observe between people in teams or in meetings. If life is not there, it's not likely to be found elsewhere. I'll describe each sign of life briefly and give examples of what we might see a group doing that shows this life at work. Keep these signs of life in perspective: They are small indicators that life is present, evidence that something vital is happening. Keep in mind a group you work with as you read through these signs. Make a few notes along the way.

Choice

Everyone chooses to be a part of the group; anyone can leave or stay. Everyone acknowledges personal responsibility. Choice reduces suspicion and increases democracy. Voluntary participation affects every significant action. A person's presence is itself an affirmation of the group. People are here because they want to be, not just for the money. In a meeting, you might hear someone ask how a pending decision would affect people's willingness to come back for another meeting. Or a member will remind others that they are each choosing to be here. Or someone will express respect for the choice members are making, the choice to be *here*.

Boundaries

Boundaries establish identity. When the boundaries of the group are very open, identity is harder to establish. When the boundaries are too closed, identity becomes inflexible and fixed. Groups struggle with issues of membership and purpose. Awareness of boundaries—what's us and what isn't—is essential to the group's sense of being. Dynamic, organic boundaries, reviewed constantly, are the prevailing choice. In group meetings, it's useful for the group members to ask what they stand for . . . and don't stand for. Or to ask each member to tell others what defines this group, what separates it from others. Or to give themselves time to make and share notes about the boundaries of the group.

Contagious Excitement

Group members can only begin to move outside the group to take action when they are excited together inside the group. Members pay attention to what people are excited about, knowing that the energy that comes with excitement is essential to whatever the group chooses to do. A key question is, "Are we excited about this among ourselves?" Projects taken on without everyone sharing the excitement are less successful than those that truly capture the heart and energy of the whole group. In meetings, group members will check to see whether everyone is excited before taking a project to the next step. When people aren't, they are asked what would cause them to get excited. Discussion recognizes the need for every member to be invested.

Learning by Doing

The group members discover who they are and what they want to do through designing it and doing it. Rather than waiting and debating, they do it and learn from the doing. They learn what works and what doesn't, what they like and what they don't. The pattern of experimentation is stronger than patterns of caution and inaction. They are open to trying anything they suspect will advance them and they can learn from quickly. In meetings, they remind themselves not to be too cautious. Or they ask what they could try out and learn from. What could they do *now*? They lean toward taking action without overplanning.

Spirit of Inquiry

Groups are at their best when a "spirit of inquiry" prevails. When members ask questions intended to expand the boundaries of their knowledge and experience, the group grows. When members show a pattern of demonstrating what they already know, the group does not grow, it calcifies. The life of the group is enhanced as the members inquire into what they are curious about, what they do not yet know, what is mysterious to them. In meetings, they will ask each other what questions are intriguing to them. Or someone will comment on how the group's energy grows when they are exploring new realms together. Or they might ask people to withhold statements or speeches they have made in the past. They come up with methods and designs that help the group explore together.

Self-Reliance

Group members look to themselves and to the resources already around them when deciding what to do next. Their first action is not to bring in an outside expert; they'd sooner figure out what they already know among themselves. They would sooner do it themselves, using and building their own abilities in the process. They pay attention to what they know and what they would like to know. In meetings, when about to take an action, someone might ask who would like to learn more about this by doing it—or who knows how to do this and would agree to helping a less experienced person do it. Or members might list what they already know that relates to the issue at hand.

Work Process

A group's deeper life is rooted in the continuing success of their internal work processes rather than in products produced and shoved out the door. Of course, external products are important in order for the group to justify its life; it's just that they are not nearly as sustaining for the group's life as the internal work done by the members. Outputs provide a place to go, but getting there—the process—is where most of the group's time is invested. The intended outcome provides common focus, direction, and movement; while having a clear process guides behavior along the way and gives the group's members a way of telling how they are doing. In meetings, members might ask how well they are working together. Or they might encourage other members to pay attention to some aspect of process, like time. Or they might comment on how encouraging or discouraging the current process is.

Direction

A surprising number of life-charged groups do not know where they are going. They are actively in search of a destination, without knowing precisely what it is at the moment. Members value traveling together as they seek a destination. In fact, the destination seems to be constantly moving—with the agreement of the group. They can cite times when they planned where to go next for the sake of what they might discover along the way. These groups demonstrate a wonderful mix of purposefulness and discovery. In meetings, members will ask again and again, where are we going? Or a member might say where she thinks the group is going and check that with others. Or someone will express discouragement about the group's lack of direction. Or the group might pause on its current path to consider how that path might be adjusted.

Leadership

In group meetings, leadership moves to the people with the most useful knowledge and skills. Even when there is an organizational hierarchy, it doesn't play out strongly. The larger group often entrusts a few people to act in the interests of all. In one meeting, you might hear someone ask which three people are willing to plan the next meeting. And that might be followed by asking the whole group to advise the planners before they go off and plan. In the next meeting, you might hear the planners offer their meeting plan and ask for the group's support or modification.

Continuity

Continuity of membership gives depth and testifies to the life of this group. The longer-term members carry the history of the group within them. They provide the confidence that the rest of the team can build upon. The group pays attention to keeping more experienced members involved and invested, drawing on their history and wisdom. In meetings, a more senior member might be asked whether what they are about to do has been done before. Or the group might give special attention to someone who over time has reliably represented a particular viewpoint.

Discontinuity

New members disturb the old order. New members bring refreshing and irritating questions, causing the group to reconsider its relevance, its purpose, or its processes; they help avoid the ruts. In meetings, you might see an older member draw out a newer one. Or you might hear someone suggest what viewpoints the group is missing—and needs. Or someone offering new and uncomfortable ideas will be reinforced for doing so. Or an old project might be given to a new member.

Connection

When a group does not meet regularly, it begins losing its identity as a group. Regular connections among the group enable a community to form. With planned meetings, the group takes itself seriously; it will explore purpose and identity and membership and action over time because it knows it will be around. In meetings, these groups identify a larger common purpose to which they are all committed. This level of purpose requires they plan on a life together that extends into the future. They discuss future work together in the context of their planned future meetings and contacts. They use all means of contact that will enrich their group life: e-mail, telephone, task teams, reading, notes—anything that keeps them connected.

All of these signs of life are immediately evident. Like a doctor with a patient, we are not trying to judge the deeper purpose of this group's life; we are not into therapy; we are just checking the pulse. And pulse is important!

Review any notes you made about the group you work with.

- What patterns emerge?
- What actions do your thoughts suggest?
- Who might you talk with about this? What would you say to them?
- What does my list of points seem to be missing?

Part Three

Finding Beauty Within the Beast

A vaudeville routine begins with an empty stage. Then stage right, you see the rear end of . . . then the whole person of . . . a clown tugging on a heavy rope, pulling it from behind the curtain across the stage. Whatever is on the other end of the rope is unseen and resisting. But the clown is making progress, loudly huffing and puffing, pulling the rope taut across the stage. The clown pulls the rope off stage left, and now you see nothing but the rope wobbling horizontal to the stage, and you hear the clown's grunting and wheezing as he continues his work offstage. The rope keeps moving to the left . . . and now you hear someone on the other end of the rope . . . and now at stage right, you see someone's feet sliding, being slowly dragged from behind the curtain by the rope . . . and now you see that the person being dragged is . . . the clown! The same clown that was on the other end of the rope. And we laugh.

And why do we laugh? Because it's nonsense, yes, but also because it is sense. We know that we are the clown; we are on both ends of the rope. We drag ourselves into new situations, into the future, toward our aspirations. We resist, holding onto what we already have. We are on both ends of the rope; we maintain that polarity within ourselves. We are the beauty; we are the beast, and it is not always clear which is which. We are the living tension, the dilemma, the paradox, the contradiction. We continue to seek resolution of the tension; we continue to maintain the tension. We live this over and over again—this is what learning and growing and living are about.

The organization is also the clown at both ends of the rope. You may have laughed with co-workers as you observed your organization tugging both ends of the rope. Or you perhaps wondered if management (the clowns?) really knew what they were doing as they instructed two departments to pull in opposite directions. And isn't it a riot when, after all of their huffing and puffing, they succeed in pulling themselves onto center stage! Some of us enjoy it, others get angry, and others lament. Others also say, "Of course, they are on the both ends of the rope."

Parts One and Two of this book defined the ends of the rope: Beast and Beauty. Part Three pulls them together, recognizing that we are on both ends of the rope, we are at once assisting and resisting, and we are creating the tension. Now, we will honor the tension and make it constructive. How do we change, transform, or renew organizations? We do it through the choices we make now, through starting where we are—the only time and place we can start from. You may recall from the fairy tale, the long struggle between Belle and the Beast as each evening he asked for her full acceptance of him and she held back, but all the while a relationship was building between them. They maintained the tension and created something from it.

"Renew" is a particularly appropriate word for the change we want to encourage: New shoots from old roots is a lovely characterization of what happens when organizations change. Though you will also be reading words like "change" and "transform," the word that best fits is "renew." When you read it, think aspiration, think ascendance, think about breathing new life into organizations—all those beautiful notions we explored in earlier chapters.

Part Three holds up twenty assertions of better ways to renew organizations. Not "truths," "principles," "guides," or "beliefs," but "assertions"—my declarations of what is required to renew large organizations. I am offering this guidance for the day-to-day choices you make. Choose to follow these twenty assertions and you will support long life for your organization. Dismiss these assertions and you will detract from that long life. That's what I am asserting; that's the measure being used. Yes, it will often conflict with those more tangible and immediate measures like this month's sales or current return on investment. I am not trying to eliminate the conflict, but broaden it and build on the new tensions created. These twenty assertions lead to organizations that thrive for generations without forgetting about what is needed this month—that's the deeper dynamic I want to help create. These assertions will help you bring the longer-life considerations to your meetings, your thinking, your choices.

There are five assertions in each of the four chapters focusing on the four "R's" of Reach, Roots, Response, and Realities:

- **Chapter 7: The Reach for Renewal.** We begin with the reach for ascendant life because it is essential to everything an organization does. Five renewal assertions guide an organization's daily awareness of the larger possible life.
- **Chapter 8: The Roots of Renewal.** Solid forward movement depends on a respectful look backward to what made the organization what it is today. Five renewal assertions elaborate on how to appreciate and use this important history today.

- **Chapter 9: The Response to Renewal.** How does an organization respond to what is going on around it in the moment? How does it move beyond reaction to thoughtful action? Five renewal assertions help the organization be more effective in the present, more reflective in the moment.
- **Chapter 10: The Realities of Renewal.** There seem to be some "givens" that need to be considered in all renewal efforts. Five renewal assertions bring together these pervasive considerations.

These twenty assertions guide practical action toward your aspirations. Keep them in mind and you will behave differently. These four chapters do not tell you what specific action to take tomorrow morning, but suggest what you should be looking for and asking about. Each assertion offers you a few ideas for perspective and a few questions for inquiry. Take the ideas to work with you, discuss the questions with others, use them in your decision making, and new actions will emerge.

Not far into my twenty assertions, you will recognize the tune I am humming. And you will see how my pattern, this tune, fits with your own implied assertions. When you are humming in harmony with what you read, how does this particular assertion fit with your own? When the sound is dissonant, where is the divergence? These four chapters offer my side of this duet; you will provide the other. Grab an end of the rope and pull—and hum along.

Chapter 7

The Reach for Renewal

What could we do to bring our dreams to life in this organization? Or how could we make it more likely that our desired future will inform the present? Here are five answers to those questions, five renewal assertions elaborated on in this chapter:

- Pursue life.
- Commit to a compelling unknown.
- Take a grand leap.
- Face the future ready to learn.
- Create irrational positive expectations.

Assertion 1
Pursue Life

The world is changed by passionate, committed people creating better lives for themselves, their families, and future generations. This is what political revolution, the women's movement, the civil rights movement, the reformation, the union movement, and educational reform have in common. Their source of energy is the larger life aspired to, worth working for now. The heart of renewal in our work organizations is just as grand, though not as romanticized. We too are pursuing our lives in these organizations; we too are reaching for a future beyond what we have experienced; we too want the work world to be better for the people who follow us. Our organizations are not renewed by people inspired by their job descriptions. No, they reach into their "life *as*criptions" to find the energy they need—the life description they ascribe to and aspire to, and their work is part of it. This is where renewal energies brew; this is how organizations are enlivened over and over again into future generations.

There is much less energy for renewal available within the formal boundaries of an organization when working entirely within its structures and systems. When the message is, "Let's create a new department by following the old rules and roles," we end up with a project straight out of *Dilbert,* breeding similar cynicism. We can't build toward our aspirations simply by upholding what we have already built. We have to risk going where those before us have not been, where we have not been. We have to imagine where we want to go and take steps in that direction.

This is a risky proposition. Encourage people to reach for what they want and they may do it! Their reach may be in directions that have nothing to do with creating a better organization and everything to do with creating better lives for themselves. This risk is worth it, but not easy when we expect to define and control the boundaries of "our" renewal project. When we avoid the risk, we miss the creative and passionate energy that people release when they see the prospect of improving their lives. To avoid the risk is to never know what we might have done together to revitalize our organization. We must choose our struggle: whether to struggle with the issues that come from helping people release their creative energies, or with the issues that come from asking people to live in their present and more predictable roles. . . . There is that rope again and we are on both ends of it.

Here are some questions to ask of people you work with:

- ✧ What do we aspire to in our lives?
- ✧ How do we currently realize our life aspirations through our work?
- ✧ What is the organization reaching for that has the promise of fulfilling people's lives?
- ✧ How do our aspirations fit with the current organizational culture?
- ✧ What opportunities are there to engage people in these questions?

Assertion 2
Commit to a Compelling Unknown

An example illustrates this assertion. An organization renewal team had been working together for six months. They were in the midst of yet another meeting to figure out how to put some visionary and risky recommendations before the entire organization of 800 people. The turning point for team agreement came when one member said, "I don't know if our proposal will be accepted. And, I don't know whether it will work. What I *do* know is that we *must* propose it! This organization must do something and this team has the opportunity to offer a new direction—even if we have to risk failing in the process!" She spoke for everyone present, and to our next assertion. Important change reaches far beyond what we have known and contains these defining elements:

- ✧ We have not been there before.
- ✧ It feels new, mysterious, and compelling.
- ✧ It is full of life for the people involved.
- ✧ We do not know whether we will be able to do it.
- ✧ We believe passionately in it.
- ✧ We are drawn forward by its possibilities.

Another story comes from the same organization a few months later—after the adoption of the renewal team's ideas: The general manager and I were having a beer after a very successful three-day meeting involving sixty people. Together they had described the ambitious future they would like to create. The GM was excited about what the group had just accomplished. He began to muse on what might happen next. And, engineer that he was, he began to chart out next steps, deciding what we ought to do next. Though laid out on four cocktail napkins, his plans were beginning to look and sound very concrete. My discomfort began to grow. I didn't want to dampen his enthusiasm, but I finally burst out, "Harry, if we knew precisely where we were going, I wouldn't want to go there!" He looked at me, puzzled and disappointed. Then he wadded up the napkins and put them aside. "I get it," he said. "It's not my job to make our future entirely predictable—that's what we always do. It's my job is to encourage this exploration and the discovery of what we might do next." What an insight!

In that three-day meeting, sixty people began creating their future together, a future that related to their whole lives, not just to their work. And they learned that their common aspirations could guide their steps, that their design would emerge step by step. Yes, there is a place for planning too, but this group discovered the aspirations that precede and bring life to plans. Pursuit of the unknown is critical to renewal.

If you are going after success that is assured because you have been there before, you are not renewing this organization, you are just redecorating. It may be important; it is not renewal. All of the unknowns are what make the mission instantly attractive to many people, but those paid for being rational and analytic may hesitate initially. Take these questions to work with you:

- ✧ What is the very best outcome we hope to see from our work together?
- ✧ What could this organization attempt that would be potentially both good for the organization and exciting to the people in it?

- Individually, what do you find compelling in what you are now doing?
- Individually, describe some projects you have participated in that were especially exciting. What made them that way?
- What would a renewal effort have to contain for you to commit strongly to it?
- How can we support continued excitement about work and renewal here?

Assertion 3
Take a Grand Leap

Renewal is not about baby steps; it is not about "transitioning" . . . or "incremental action" . . . or "evolving." None of these has the ring of renewal about it. Step boldly from the well-known present toward an unexplored, fascinating future. Possibility plus risk creates excitement, the grandness of a leap that is larger than the costs and pain that will come with it. Being magnetically drawn toward the future *and* anxious about how to get there—these are the life-giving elements needed. The dream and the reality are compelling in combination, because of the huge gap between. People stand on the edge, wanting to make the leap and wondering if they can make it, leaning out while holding back. Then they make the choice to leap.

Grand leaps like this do not happen over a weekend. These leaps stretch out for years. Big dreams require this kind of reach. In fact, the reach must extend beyond the people who started it for it to be truly great. It will involve new workers, the next generation, and generations beyond. It must be larger than those of us who happen to be around at the moment. With the huge dream comes huge demands. Examine your renewal efforts at work:

- What would be truly a great and scary leap forward for this organization?
- What do people find most compelling about making this great leap?

- What frightens people about the leap?
- What could you choose to do together to prepare you for this leap?

Most of the important steps we take are small and sequential and necessary. These organizational refinements must continue; they are the important day-to-day learning and adjustment required within all organizations. And they are not what we have been considering here.

Assertion 4
Face the Future Ready to Learn

Helping an organization move toward a future it has never experienced requires humility and openness. If you are committed to guiding people toward a new vision, you will be humbled frequently. If you are a person who needs to know "first and most," you probably will take advantage of the numerous opportunities to embarrass yourself. Lack of humility is a great block to progress.

Two personal examples: I was beginning work with a new client, a marketing company. From the start, I knew what they needed. How fortunate for them to have me! I knew that we could make changes around here faster because of my success elsewhere. You can imagine what that approach did for me—and that is not the worst of it! Since I "knew," I didn't have to ask. . . . In fact, I couldn't ask. Since I was "experienced" and they weren't, I expected deference. Since I was "wise," I expected them to listen. My nearsightedness cost the client and the project critical time. I was not open to learning. I took an aggressive stance and blamed them when things went wrong. This was not fun work for me to do. It was even less fun for them.

Contrast that work with my experience on a project in my community: I helped conceive this project and joined five others in shaping its direction. Then the six of us reached out to the larger community for support. As citizens began showing up, I became more aware of how much experience I had that was potentially useful to the project and to the newly involved citizens. I also became aware of how little they knew about doing this kind of work. So far, I sound something like my earlier description with a dash of tolerance. But something had shifted and I approached this citizen community differently. I still knew what I knew, but I recognized that there was much they knew that I needed to learn. I saw this as a special opportunity for me. Instead of using my time to brag about what I already knew, I tried to find out more about them and what we were doing together. I have special talents—and they do too. I made a point of delving into their experience—and they brought so much! We succeeded in creating the project together, each of us with an openness to what the future might hold and the readiness to influence it.

Initially, it was hard to ask and listen, rather than to show and tell; hard to gather information; rather than to demonstrate how much I knew. But this is the receptiveness and humility that deep learning demands. Approaching the work with new eyes, the eyes of a novice, was what served the work well. And that is my repeated experience. I say "repeated" because my ego has made sure that I have had to learn this lesson over and over again. Each time, I rediscover how essential humility is to my learning and effectiveness. And here are questions for you to take to work:

- How does this organization uphold the importance of learning?
- Where have we seen leaders valuing humility?
- What do we need to learn? What are our key unanswered questions?
- How might we show a readiness to learn in the midst of renewal?

Assertion 5

Create Irrational Positive Expectations

For our work in renewal to have any chance of lasting, it must be drawn forward by the dreams of participants. Their hopes for the future and the trust they place in each other are all justified in positive expectations yet to be realized.

Hope and trust are close cousins, often traveling in each other's company, leaning expectantly toward the future. When one is absent, the other often is too. Hope is a delicate and important indicator of how the renewal effort is doing now; it is the felt connection between present activity and life purpose. Hopeful people believe that their actions support better lives for themselves and others important to them. They are positive about the future and helping to create it. When renewal is succeeding, the hopes of many people align toward common purpose. When despair appears, alignment is scattered and renewal is in trouble.

Trust is that slippery keystone that renewal efforts lean upon. Without trust, people will not attempt new work together; they will not venture or risk willingly. We build trust by doing things together over time. Two of us might be working together, shoulder to shoulder, seeing what the other sees, knowing what we each do and how we do it, experiencing each other's decisions, emotions and aspirations. We grow to trust each other based on our positive, shared history of mutual interest and action. When what we do together works, our trust deepens. Through shared activities, we each put down the small roots of an entwined relationship. More mutual action means more roots. Multiply us by three and we now have a team of six with a positive shared history of mutual interest and action, and more intertwined roots . . . and you can see where this is headed. With time, the bonds of shared history and partnership can make us an effective, almost inseparable work group.

Both hope and trust require vulnerability. When I trust you, I have confidence in you, I am betting on you . . . and you could disappoint me. If you could not, then trust is not involved. When I am hopeful about the future, I am expectant, I am investing myself in its possibilities . . . and I could be disappointed. If I have nothing invested in that future, then hope is not involved. Trust, hope, and vulnerability go together. None of them has the tangible qualities that we so often use to measure how an organization is doing, but everyone recognizes the ambiance in an organization that has them (or lacks them). A reach for a new organizational future will not succeed without them.

Our organizational renewal efforts often expect people to trust and be hopeful more quickly than is possible. There are no trust potions or hope prescriptions that cause others to bond quickly, with high expectations for the future. The process is more biological than mechanical and it doesn't happen overnight—regardless of the needs of the organization. New leaders are usually amazed at how long it takes to create authentic, lasting change. It takes time to build trust and nurture hope.

When cooking up renewal, we are stirring ingredients—including the workers—into a mixture that we only partially understand. We created a recipe and are using it for the first time. We know what we intend, but we don't know exactly what we are creating or exactly what will happen. We are asking others to trust us, to be hopeful about the outcome, and to risk—be vulnerable—during the process. That is a lot to ask, but we do it for the sake of the better future that many of the people involved aspire to . . . which leads to a caution: There is a good chance our renewal recipe will not turn out as we intended; it usually doesn't. Remember that the people we asked to trust, to be hopeful and vulnerable, live in this organization; they will still be here long after this renewal effort has finished. Build trust, and nurture hope, as if you were going to be living in this organization the rest of your life. Here are some questions to take back to work with you:

- ✧ Describe successful work experiences in which trust and hope were essential elements.
- ✧ What does trust mean to us? How do we demonstrate it?
- ✧ How do we build trust among people who need it to work together?
- ✧ How does trust figure into our current projects?

- ✧ What is the hope or fulfillment that brings people to work each day?
- ✧ How do people hope their work here will support their lives beyond work?

This chapter has focused on the reach for a new future. Pair these thoughts with those expressed in Part Two where we explored the beauty of the beast. Give particular attention to the eight aspirations in Chapter 5; imagine how you could connect those aspirations to the five assertions in this chapter. Think about how you might engage fellow workers in questions that help them lean toward the future.

Chapter 8

The Roots of Renewal

A few comments heard in the midst of organization renewal: "We'd be better off to just burn this place down and start over!" . . . "I have *no* idea how an organization so screwed up made it so far!" . . . "These people are completely unprepared to make this place work!" Note the implications about the organization and its people. Many efforts at creating new life in organizations operate from the assumption that this place is dead—or ought to be. What it needs is not renewal, but resurrection . . . or miracles from godlike leaders—a role appealing to many of us.

Starting over is not an option. We are here to help an established organization move in new directions. Imagining another starting point provides temporary diversion, but little else. This is the organization; this is where we begin. And this chapter will help us respect what the organization brings to this moment: history. It is that rich soil in which the seeds of renewal will root. We will explore these five assertions:

- Renewal takes root in the past.
- New effort relies on old resources.

- Change doesn't make sense.
- We fall back on the familiar.
- We spend years preparing not to change.

These assertions are all about discovering and respecting the organization you serve. If you are in an old organization, you are working with people who have been here for years. They have learned a great deal about the life of this place; they *are* the life of this place. It may not be the life that you (or they) aspire to, but it is life nevertheless. This old life will nourish the seeds of the new life you will be trying to grow. Or this old life will provide the humus in which the new seeds are planted. In either case, the life of this old place is vital to whatever comes next.

Assertion 6

Renewal Takes Root in the Past

Agricultural metaphors are particularly appropriate to organizations. Their fertile, earthy, organic substance grounds those of us working in glass towers fourteen floors above dirt. So don your bib overalls and recognize that today and tomorrow are rooted in yesterday. We must do more than respect the past; we must sink our renewal's roots into it. Perhaps this is more than a metaphor; perhaps we are tending an underlying natural growth process. Maybe we are farmers and don't know it.

That past is embodied in people who have been here through it all and who are proud of what they have done. They have been essential to what the organization has accomplished so far, and most of them will be part of what happens next. People with roots have deeper loyalties than those who have just arrived. Many of us are critical of these stubborn, attached, traditional workers. When it comes to creating change, they are often seen as major barriers. And damned frustrating they are!

Yet, some of the largest and most successful change efforts I've witnessed have had the support of the rooted population—not that it usually started out that way. No, it takes months of work with the people who have history here—frustrating, hard work because they are holding onto what they have spent years learning and succeeding in. It is a challenge to use the past in building the future, but any renewal effort that disrespects this ingrained history is in for trouble.

In mature organizations, the majority who have invested for the long haul represent what this organization is about, like it or not. These folks "know" where this company is going and determinedly take it there—whether the management shares that knowledge or not. They are the strategy in action, regardless of what leaders are expressing. These people know what is important to them and pursue it without talking about it. A newcomer may have difficulty getting them to discuss it, but their silence is not ignorance. They are investing in their security, their pension, and their future. They have decided, and they intend to stick with their decision as the future unfolds.

Renewal efforts can also get terminally tied up in the old ways of doing things. Each decision gets dealt with in the same old committee structure or assigned to the same old people. Watch out. Renewal carried out through entrenched processes doesn't work. Years have been invested in creating these old ways that will discard ideas that threaten the processes in place. A common example is the organizations structured around functions (sales, operations, research, marketing) that reject any ideas that suggest structuring around the products that flow through these functions.

Here lies the dilemma you face in each moment of a renewal effort: respecting what has gone before while creating what will happen next. Live in that dilemma. Do not put yourself on one side or the other, but keep it alive in yourself and in the people around you. This dilemma lives in the discussions held, the future imagined, and the past respected, assuring a deeper consideration of how to best renew this place. Questions useful in this dynamic include:

- What are the essential values and purposes that made us what we are, without which we would cease to be?

- ✧ Which of these are most important to our future?
- ✧ How are we supporting the continuation of these from our past into our future?
- ✧ Who would be important to engage in this effort?

Assertion 7
New Effort Relies on Old Resources

This assertion is a corollary to the last one. Have you ever been part of a renewal program that was announced like this: "Things are going to change around here. . . . We are going to move in new directions. . . . You will need all new skills. . . . All those ways you've been doing things for years? Forget 'em. . . . Cast out the old; bring in the new. . . . A new day has dawned. . . . You once were lost, but now you're found. . . . Praise change." Does this sound familiar to you? I hear it as, "To be valued around here, forget your medieval skills and learn these brand-new skills." This approach is both wrong and demoralizing.

When the change effort is in place and we look around at who is making it work, who do we see? Mostly, we see the very people we called together to motivate at the beginning. In other words, the effort is succeeding because of the abilities of people who have been here and will be here for some time. Those old and reliable resources are the backbone of this new effort. Yes, they add new skills to old, but usually those additions are a small portion of what they are relying on for success. Mostly, they rely on what they have learned over the years. Far from casting those old skills and abilities aside, this renewal effort builds on this old base and could not succeed without it.

I'm recalling a renewal effort in which changes were getting sullen resistance from a number of older, experienced employees—and their resistance was spreading to other employees who respected the more experienced folks. We asked the group to sort themselves out by years of experience, most to least. Then we asked those long in experience to tell stories to the rest of us, stories about what they liked about working here twenty-plus years ago. The stories were many, long, and wonderful. And moving. Afterwards, the group agreed that what it wanted to create now had many of the elements of what these old-timers has experienced. At that point, resistance shifted toward support.

For our renewal to succeed, we must reinforce what people already know and do what fits with the future form of the company. This existing knowledge, skill, and spirit was carefully constructed over years; new life will grow from this. Disparaging it is a grand show of ignorance; recognizing it is the beginning of wisdom. Consider:

- Tell stories from the old days that express what we want to have here today.
- What special experience and abilities, connections and culture, have we developed over the years?
- What from the past is important to our future?
- How could we retain and reinforce these abilities and qualities in the organization?
- What could we do to make sure our renewal efforts respect the individuals that represent the history of this place?

Assertion 8
Change Doesn't Make Sense

Listen in on two employees getting their first briefing on a new work process: "You have each been working here for about five years. You've done a good job . . . but now the company has come up with a new way for you to approach your work. We are calling it The ACCEL Process; it tells you better ways to do your job. After we work through ACCEL with you—since participation is key—you will learn new ways of doing your job." Imagine their reactions and the looks on their faces. For five years this company has been encouraging them to do their jobs in just the way they are doing them today. Thousands of times, they found reinforcement for thinking, "This is the way to do my job." And when ACCEL comes along, should it be a surprise to us that they do not leap for joy? No, and why not? Because from where they sit, change does not make sense. What makes sense is continuing to refine what they have been doing, to get better and better at it.

Change asks people to release their hold on what makes sense to them. They have been doing this for years; now we want them to do something else. The call to change brings up feelings and reactions. But who isn't upset when their long-established and successful ways of working are put aside for something new? Few people regularly look for the opportunity to give up their established routines. Most people prefer the predictability of what they have been doing and resent the interruption. This is not a matter of how they "should" feel, or how I want them to respond; it's a matter of how they are. And that must be respected.

The same people who are holding onto their established ways of working may be signing up for evening classes in conversational Spanish or woodworking or line dancing. Why is it that change is attractive in the evening and resisted at work? Again, it is not about sense; it's about motivation: Who is motivated to change? When the ACCEL program was introduced, management was motivated to seek change, not the workers. With the evening classes, the participants are choosing to sign up. For change to work smoothly, it must be chosen. Of course we can force it on people, but we will live with the consequences. Consider these questions back at work:

- What changes are considered "nonsense" to the people whose work will be changed? How would they express that?
- What makes sense to the people working here? How would they express that?
- How does the organization appreciate its people's contributions, experience, service, and loyalty?
- How could we engage affected people in the early stages of renewal?

- ✧ What could we do to help people feel good about themselves while changes are taking place in their work?

Assertion 9

We Fall Back on the Familiar

When we do not understand, we rely on what is comfortable for us, what we are familiar with, what we can control, what we have done in the past—even if it is not working now. At least that seems to be the more common pattern among us.

A manager called last week and spoke of her months of overwork on a "fire" that she has yet to quench. And the fire shows no signs of abating. While she dampens this portion of it, it blazes up somewhere else. She has to do something; she is doing what she knows how to do; she knows it isn't working; and she continues. I'm reminded of the television news showing the burning house, the homeowner with a garden hose spraying a puny stream of water into the consuming flames. This homeowner had to do something; he was doing what he knew how to do; he knew it wasn't working; and he continued. Many organizations take the same approach when working on an issue larger than their present comprehension or skills. They bring old and familiar tools and skills to this immensely unfamiliar and larger problem. People work into the night wielding old tools on new "fires."

Our commitment to what is familiar can separate us from what is possible. It's hard to let go of the way I have been behaving for years. To let go could mean that I have been doing it wrong . . . or that I am not as good as I think I am . . . or that you are unhappy with my work . . . or that you are unhappy with me . . . or that you no longer like me. And the list goes on into all of those other anxieties and insecurities we can activate when old, familiar ways are not working. Take these thoughts back to work with these questions:

- ✧ What are some of the old and familiar ways of this organization?

- Describe experiences in which we relied on old ways past their usefulness.
- What are the organization's reactions when established ways are challenged?
- What are we doing to demonstrate our openness to new ways?
- How do we help people step back from the familiar to consider effectiveness?

Assertion 10
We Spend Years Preparing Not to Change

Imagine a room full of accountants who have been working separately, and quite successfully, for seven years. You've got a plan that would cause them to assist each other in getting the work done. It's a good plan; it would enrich their work; it would serve customers better; it would cost less; and it would even make the accountants happier, more fulfilled people. You *know* this—and you *know* you are right!

These accountants have spent at least seven years preparing *not* to accept your plan. They have found working alone rewarding enough that they have not quit. They have each shown up for work for 1800 days and done their jobs just like they did the day before. They have created informal systems and social groups; they have norms for dealing with each other; they have "in" jokes that relate to their work, their bosses, the company, and each other. No, they are not consciously saying, "We want to keep doing just what we have been doing the way we have been doing it for seven years." But showing up for years is determining them to do what they already doing: They have been preparing for years *not* to do what you are now proposing.

This is reality, not to be cursed, but accepted. When you offer this great opportunity, and the accountants go, "Huh?" this is your opportunity to say to yourself, "Well, of course! They have spent years moving and learning in a direction different from what I am suggesting. And the department has rewarded them for being predictable in doing the work as the department wanted it done." And you could say further to yourself, "No, I am not going to rail against them because they are stuck in old ways and cannot see the brilliance of the future I am offering. No, I am going to stop and learn about what they have been doing for years and how they feel about it because *that* is my starting point for engaging them in thinking about new ways of designing their work." Yes, you could say all of that to yourself. But will you?

In truth, we are the accountants. Over time, we are each choosing our best way of doing things. Whether it is writing a report or brushing our teeth, we gradually come up with our best ways in areas of life and work, which we repeat. We reduce them to habit so we can turn our heads and hands loose to work on other things. And we don't deal easily with someone intruding with a new and better way. When someone comes along with a different way of doing things, we don't want to let go of our carefully honed ways; we have spent years refining them, years preparing not to let go of them, years of learning them deeply. Here are some questions to open the subject at work:

- ✧ What have we made into habits in the way we approach our work?
- ✧ How are our habits valuable to us?
- ✧ What is our reaction when people suggest we change what we've been doing for years?
- ✧ What are some examples of habits we used to have that we have replaced? What caused us to change?
- ✧ How could we reconsider work habits to make sure they serve us well?

The beginning of this chapter discussed the past as the soil in which renewal efforts are rooted. Our five assertions have tilled that soil from different directions, reinforcing themes of learning and respect as we found value in history. Those of us invested in renewal need to look back into the organization at the very moment we are asking others to look forward.

Chapter 9

The Response to Renewal

Enough of the roots in the past; enough of the reach to the future—it's time to discuss the present. How do we respond in this moment—that fraction of time that every other moment is known through? How do we breathe life into this moment? What do we do *now*? This chapter offers five answers to these questions, assertions to guide your responses to the renewal opportunities that come up again and again. Use these guides to stimulate your own beliefs about the stance you take toward work as it confronts you every day. Here are the headlines:

- There is no right answer.
- Find the creative tension.
- Make the complex simple.
- Create informed choice.
- Engage everyone.

These five assertions are more immediate than those we reviewed earlier; these live in the moment. You can remind yourself of them while you are listening to others or making a point of your own. You can use these points to assess how you are communicating in a meeting right now. These are empowering assertions—for you and for the people you are working with. The assertions help you seek clarity and progress.

Assertion 11
There Is No Right Answer

There is no one answer; there are no answers; there are many answers; there is no right answer—all are permutations of the same difficult truth. This is a hard assertion to argue for (partly because it is itself an answer), with all of us schooled in getting the right answer and getting it first. But experience doesn't seem to bear out what we learn in school. Years of organizational change projects show that 60 to 80 percent of organizational change efforts fail to achieve what they set out for. Most of those efforts thought they had "the" answer. Yet we continue to create organizations that do not work well. Despite all of the talent and resources we pour into them, we haven't found the compelling, right way. Our more enlightened self may say, "Of course not!" and our less enlightened self says, "Damn!"

We may know there are many answers and no one right answer. Yet we continue to search, our appetite for new change methods—whether personal or organizational—seems insatiable. Diets, exercise equipment, self-help books, and seminars are selling like never before. All this intensity appears to be a search for the one right answer. Our fast-moving and greedy marketplace convinces us we are coming up short, fat, or unproductive—and it has the answers we need. The way to our own answers is noisy and confusing; there is no clear, smooth path to truth.

We deal with this clamoring for our attention and money both within ourselves and within our organizations. The resolving turns first on our aspirations: What kind of world are we creating? We must choose among alternatives, knowing that there are many answers, with no one right answer, and we will create an answer that works. These questions could stimulate interesting discussion with co-workers:

- How do we describe the situation that surrounds us? What, if any, common description do we agree upon?
- How does our way of working together keep us open to information we might need?
- How do we choose? What's the process? How does it work?
- Describe experiences in which we have created good alternatives and made good choices together.
- How do we go about creating answers together?

Assertion 12
Find the Creative Tension

Our work on renewal is in the gap between reality and possibility. There is always a tension in the difference between:

- the ways things are and the way they should be or could be.
- our realizations and our aspirations.
- what we want and what we've got.
- organizational plans and visions.

The fact that there is a difference is not enough; there must be an important difference—that's where creative tension is possible. The gap must create a tension in each person doing the work. If the gap is there, but no one cares, no tension means no action. An early test of renewal efforts is whether the creative tension level is high enough among those involved. We can help people create or discover the gap, and how important it is to them. We can help the various parties understand how the tensions they feel are similar to and different from each other. We can help them gauge what they might want to do together. We watch for differences between what people have and what they want, the gap necessary to motivated action.

These questions help highlight the importance of creative tension at work:

- If creative tension is defined as an important gap between what we've got and what we want, what are important gaps we are now working with?
- How do this organization's aspirations, values, or goals figure in the gaps we've got around here? What's been done to clarify the gaps with people who care?
- Tell about an experience in which this organization did a fine job of helping everyone understand a gap that needed concerted action.
- Give examples of how the gaps of various groups within this organization are different.

Assertion 13
Make the Complex Simple

Imagine you are a leader of a renewal effort and standing in front of a group of people from one organization: Eighty people from seven states and six divisions, representing five functions and four levels of the hierarchy. Three thousand more people work for those in this room. Imagine it. . . . Now, how many actions could this group of eighty agree upon during the next two hours? Forty-three? Twenty-seven? Ten? Two? None? My bet is less than ten—and probably closer to two. And this is with just these eighty people, not even considering what's needed with the other three thousand.

If you have ever helped design renewal efforts, you know how complex they can be. Those in charge often feel the need to tell everyone everything, to sell people on their models, systems, disciplines, and terminology, as in, "This is the model that we will be using from now on, and this morning we will learn how its twelve boxes interact." Or "With this change come new words essential to expressing our direction. We've got seventeen terms we will be using, starting with 'AT' for Assimilation Terminology. . . ." There is much that makes sense about this approach. The problem is, it makes more sense than people do. It deals with people as vessels to be filled, and ignores their need for involvement, respect, and commitment. No approach works when focused only on injection of facts. Yes, change is complex, but the way to get understanding and support starts closer to what people presently understand and are committed to. When you create and offer simple next steps, building from where people are, you are more likely to succeed with them. Whenever you do not, you will face reluctance, resistance, and confusion.

The way to renewal is counterintuitive: make the complex simple. That's "simple," not "simplistic." Proponents of profound processes proclaim this cannot be done! They insist on educating everyone before installing their process—and then when it does not work, blaming everyone for not understanding. Our organizations have done this thousands of times (and will do it thousands more) criticizing those employees who can't learn, or don't want to learn, or both. Hiring hundreds of smarter, willing people is the tempting, implied solution to the problem, but it's not likely—even if they were available. The nature of renewing most organizations is that we will work with what is there. Creating a new organization with new people who have never worked together before is quite a different matter—and not our focus here.

What can you do to make the complex simple?

Show the big picture. Complex processes are more easily understood when people can see the larger picture within which all the pieces will eventually fit. When they understand the larger intention, or the underlying assumptions, or even the time path, they have something to slip the pieces into. Without a container these pieces are inclined to bounce around or fall out of place because people will not know how to relate to them.

Separate into simpler slices. Part of making the complex simple is cutting it into digestible pieces. Think carefully about how to divide the project into pieces that people can incorporate into their present experience.

Provide needed learning. Everyone does not need to know everything. Avoid dipping everyone in the same vat; favor tailoring content to work role. This is not to suggest secrecy, but effectiveness.

Offer knowledge when needed. Don't dump a truckload of knowledge on people holding out buckets. Instead, send knowledge out in buckets just when it is needed.

With co-workers, consider what you have seen happen at work:

- Give examples of projects or programs that did a wonderful job of making the complex simple. How and why were they able to do this?
- How have people in the organization reacted to past change projects? What can you learn from this?
- Select a current project and ask: What is the big picture? What are the smaller slices? What are the appropriate groups? What is the best timing?

Those of us closer to the center of change often forget how much time we have spent creating our own understanding. Our work on the project builds our commitment while we are building our understanding. We know at a deeper level what this is all about, but that is not where we must start as we try to create similar support in the rest of the organization. Start where people are right now, with what they know and want. Build from there.

Assertion 14
Create Informed Choice

A major challenge in renewal is creating alternatives from which people willingly and knowingly choose; then their choice has commitment behind it. A number of factors need to be taken into account for informed choice to happen:

Understanding. People need to appreciate the big picture we talked about earlier; they need to know how it relates to them. They need to understand the gap and feel its tension. If people cannot "get their heads around" the gap, it won't create the necessary tension. They may go through the motions, but that does not equate with understanding and enthusiasm.

Alternatives. If they have developed an array of alternatives themselves, they will be more committed to what they eventually choose. Your task is to help them develop alternatives, not to come up with alternatives yourself.

Choice. With as full an understanding as possible, the people affected must willingly choose among the alternatives they have developed.

Commitment. As a direct result of working through the other steps, everyone involved is committed to following through on their choice.

These four elements are present in all decisions a group makes, whether we are aware of it or not. Even when all four elements seem to be violated, they are still present. When decisions are made under conditions of low understanding, few alternatives, no choice, and low commitment, the disappointing outcomes testify to the importance of engaging people. We often make choices under less-than-ideal circumstances and have to live with the consequences. Improve the results by increasing involvement in the choice.

Informed choice is much more than a work or renewal tool; it is an empowering approach to life. People feel more vital and more powerful when they have understanding, alternatives, choice, and commitment. It's wonderful when that power goes to work supporting the organization. Discuss these questions at work:

- What organizational examples best demonstrate the informed choice process?
- What does the organization do best in the understanding, alternatives, choice, and commitment sequence described on the previous page? And where does it most need to improve?
- Tell of work experiences where you had informed choice. How did you feel about it?
- How could we expand people's array of choices?

Assertion 15

Engage Everyone

This is more in the nature of a command than an assertion—and it means just what it says: *everyone!* Renewal teams, management, leaders—everyone affected must be involved. In fact, everyone affected *is* involved—it's just a question of how constructive their involvement will be. The extra work of renewal when we involve everyone is immense! Why do it? Because experience repeatedly shows that *not* involving everyone does not work. We have tried every other way and just haven't found a good alternative. No, everyone does not have to be involved in the same way and with the same depth at every step; but by not involving them, we are throwing hurdles in our own path. Here are three common involvement issues:

- We choose not to involve everyone affected because we just don't have time. We'd like to, but the schedule or the budget dictates that we cannot . . . and the results are predictable: They will start talking about our actions and assumptions. They will see our actions as controlling; they will know that we assume that we know best.
- Often management expects others in the organization to change. And those "others" expect management to change. The renewal effort is depleted by lopsided expectations and mutual criticisms.

- Too often we begin changes that a few people understand—and then we blame the rest for not understanding. Those of us excited about the change forget what it took to move us to this level of understanding and commitment; and we forget how influential we were in the changes coming. We fail to provide an opportunity for all involved to understand, influence, and commit.

It is easier to help an organization agree that it needs to transform itself than it is for individuals to take the necessary action. It is not a matter of figuring out *who* ought to change, but of *how* each person will change—top to bottom, side to side, executive to worker. When you believe this, you will approach each decision with the intent of engaging each person in supporting actions. Renewal will happen through the actions we take today. Here are some engaging questions to pursue at work:

- What are the underlying assumptions about who ought to be engaged in change in your organization?
- Tell of a successful renewal experience—here or somewhere else—that engaged everyone in the organization in making change.
- How would renewal efforts currently under way be different if suddenly it was required that all affected people be involved and take action?

Summary

As we said at the beginning of the chapter, these five assertions are especially useful in the moment. Imagine yourself in a meeting of people important to a renewal project you are working on. Imagine asking questions of yourself or the group: Are we really open to all of the possibilities? What is the difference between what we've got and what we want? How can we simplify this so everyone can understand? What information do people need in order to choose? How do we assure that everyone leaves here committed to at least one action? These assertions respond to what is going on in the moment and move work forward; they convert aspirations for the future into action in the present.

Chapter 10

The Realities of Renewal

Have you noticed how your work organization is beginning to resemble a major airport? It is always under construction, always reconfiguring itself, always creating special passageways for the regular work and customers to pass through. Gradually, we are becoming adjusted to the fact that our airports will never be finished. And our freeways. And our school system. And our health care systems. And our organizations. "The good old days" when organizations were more predictable and stable are remembered by an older and shrinking population. Current expectations center on adaptation. Skills needed from now on include adapting to our surroundings, scanning ourselves and adjusting to what we find, reconsidering who we are in a new context, and shifting our boundaries. To live is to adapt while maintaining core purpose, to remain the same while becoming different. That's what organisms are about; that's what organizations are about; that's what we individuals are about.

This chapter examines the less tangible realities that determine whether we see tangible results. Earlier chapters dealt with the reach for aspirations, the roots in the past, and responding in the present; this chapter alerts us to the underpinning realities of renewal work; all five assertions deal with dynamics created by any change, whether renewing or regressing:

- We will be asked for more than we offered.
- Sustaining renewal is always the challenge.
- Renewal requires loss.
- "If it's worth doing, it's worth doing slowly."
- We make renewal happen here and now.

These assertions create frustration as you attempt to honor them, but not as much as when you forget them.

Assertion 16
We Will Be Asked for More Than We Offered

During a corporate meeting of 200 managers, I asked who would like to lose five pounds. Almost all of their hands went up. Then I asked the group to consider what we would have to do together to get 80 percent of the group to lose and not regain five pounds. What kind of effort would we have to go through? How many times would we have to meet? Over how many years? How many before-and-after cases would we have to applaud? How many prizes would we have to award? How many success stories would we have to hear? What would it take to sustain that loss of 800 pounds of fat from our collective body? The feeling in the meeting was . . . heavy. This small weight loss would require a large and concerted effort!

Compare that weight-losing effort to the ambitions we have for our organizations. Which is more complex for an organization of 200 people to do: lose 800 pounds to make themselves healthier, or redesign their organization to make themselves more productive? Substitute your most recent project for "redesign their organization" and you will still get the same result: Losing 800 pounds is not easy, but it is simple compared to most organizational renewal efforts. Our renewal ambitions could be guided by our experiences with "simpler" life change: Whatever level of effort we initially offer, the change effort will ask more of us. I've yet to be involved in a renewal effort where we all grasped the magnitude of what we were attempting.

We continue to create and commit to change that we do not understand; that is the nature of the beast. We are preparing to go somewhere we have never been. But at least we can know that we don't know; we can build this consideration into our preparation. We do not just overlook this step; we avoid it. Our planning and controlling ways do not want to acknowledge that when we move into unexplored territory we will not know what we are doing, so we build plans that give the appearance of control. We meet and reinforce each other's need to know what will happen next with plans based on our previous experiences. And of course, when we really do step into this new territory, we find it resembles—but is also quite different from—what we have known before. And invariably, it takes more energy and resources than we could anticipate. Some of us miscalculate the demands of change almost intentionally. We fear that if everyone in the organization knew now what would be required, they would not undertake it. We try to sneak by this barrier by downplaying the difficulties or waxing enthusiastic about the goals we aspire to.

Defectors from the project usually leave when the renewal is struggling during implementation. As it falters, doubts surface in statements like, "If we had known what we were getting into in the first place, we never would have started this." You have heard this same statement voiced about love matches, work projects, graduate degrees, diets, home remodeling, you name it. Having underestimated the effort needed in the beginning, we consider pulling out when we are tested. This inevitable test can be anticipated with questions like these:

- ✧ Describe in some detail what this organization will have to invest for this project to succeed.
- ✧ Consider large projects lasting over years: What made them more and less successful?

- ✧ Where are the points this project will most likely be seriously tested?
- ✧ What could we do to increase our acceptance of the fact that this project will be tested, will falter?
- ✧ How will we deal with others in the organization when this project is faltering?

Face up to the difficulty of revitalizing an organization. Avoid the discouragement and despair that comes to those who didn't anticipate the difficulty of where they were going Help yourself and your organization toward awareness of what they are getting into.

Assertion 17

Sustaining Renewal Is Always the Challenge

This assertion links closely with the last, but from a longer-term perspective. Let's assume that you and your associates have been part of a renewal project that is working. Early success patterns and results show it. The organization's members know it. Wonderful! But creating success today is not the same as continuing it—and that is what this work is really after: sustained life. Our persistent challenge is sustaining the life we have helped renew. This is one of the *most* challenging parts of our work: How do we help people find a dynamic balance around their renewed center?

This work of sustaining organizational change and renewal requires discipline and persistence that we seldom anticipate near the beginning. What most of us see as the groundbreaking and exciting work of renewal is early in the effort. There is a freshness, a fever, and often a frenzy that people are drawn to—parallel to the early days of a romance. Then the freshness and fever fade and time begins to test the effort. This is essential in the maturation of the renewal work effort—and it is not exciting. Many people desert the effort here, heading off to a new change/love that promises what this old change/love has failed to deliver. We may be among those deserters; this is a good time to consider what we really expect in our relationship with this organization.

There are other personal life parallels. Consider your own actions to change your financial habits or your health profile. It was exciting to buy the book, the software, or the equipment, but it turns out you actually have to use them *each day of the rest of your life!* Hardly fair, is it? We help our organizations launch themselves on their own health programs. Do we share their hope that this can be quick and easy? Are we reluctant to learn that it is not? Do our patterns show a search for the easy way through? Do we jump from one organizational fitness program to another, year after year? Many of us do, but if we can stand back far enough to see our patterns, perhaps we can learn from them. Consider with your fellow workers the differences between initiating and sustaining renewal. Ask:

- ✧ What are past examples of initiating and sustaining change efforts here?
- ✧ How do we help ourselves and others understand the differences between initiating and sustaining a change effort?
- ✧ How do our efforts in initiating a renewal effort need to differ from our efforts in sustaining it?
- ✧ What are systems, structures and norms of this organization that affect the renewal we wish to sustain? How might we learn more about them? How might we affect them?

Assertion 18

Renewal Requires Loss

What an abrupt, hard reality this is. With renewal comes the loss of patterns, relationships, security, and identity. This loss comes from both giving up the familiar and stepping into an uncertain future. "Oh yes, we have seen the plans, but what will *really* happen?" Renewal irrevocably disrupts the structure, systems, roles, information flow, decision making, proximity, power structure, and culture. For a while, the organization does not know what it is or what it is becoming. And the same is true for many people in it. The elements that formerly held the organization together are twisted, transfigured, and challenged to move in new directions. People are at a loss as to what to do. Of course it is uncomfortable, confusing, and resisted. The felt impact of change varies with each of us. We have created our own organizational map and we respond uniquely to having it altered, crumpled, torn, or replaced. Childhood learning about how to respond to loss rises up, attempting to exert its emotional control over our actions. We do not determine the amount, nature, and depth of hurt that is felt by each person. What one finds exciting can be devastating to another.

Many of us "experienced" in change turn ourselves away from these uncomfortable realities of organizational renewal. Years of immersion in its chaotic processes make us immune to the anxieties that others are experiencing. Our actions suggest that we expect others to react as we react—though it took us years to build this capability. While that capability shields us from much of the emotional wrenching that comes with change, it can also isolate us from the people most important to the effort. We are more effective when we open ourselves to the natural reactions that come with the loss of familiar ways and a change to new ways—each and every time.

We can do our best to see that the discomfort people feel comes from struggling with the right issues. For example, a restaurant chain changed the focus of a field manager's time, requiring weekly visits to restaurants with the lowest sales. The field managers soon were complaining that management was both reducing their latitude and increasing their travel time. They were working harder than ever and doing a less effective job than before and they were unhappy about it. Management knew the change would be painful, but this was not the kind of pain they were expecting. The hurt was coming from struggling with the wrong issues: increased manager travel time became the focus, rather than increased restaurant performance.

Contrast that with an internal project team behind in its work for their agency. In order to pull their data together, create a report, build recommendations, and plan a meeting, they poured a huge amount of energy in at the last minute. They all worked past midnight on Monday night to be ready for a Tuesday morning presentation. Their suffering was directly related to their choices and their work; they were creating a product that they were all proud of. It hurt for the right reasons.

With your co-workers, look at the consequences of renewal:

- Tell stories of organizational change that involved hard sacrifice—which was worth it.
- What personal experiences have you had that involved loss and pain necessary to accomplishment or happiness?
- How could we learn more about the value of working through the painful parts of change?
- What could we do to make it more likely that people will embrace change, given that it will not be easy for them?

Assertion 19
"If It's Worth Doing, It's Worth Doing Slowly"

And what great organization scholar do you think said that first? I am borrowing it from . . . Mae West! Yes, she was a great observer of organizations. We will use her provocative proposition as our excuse to think about the pace and intensity of renewal.

Most large systems renewal efforts are moving too fast. Competing consultants (external and internal) feed the needs of potential clients for quick and painless results. The reality of renewal is hard to sell when others offer more change for less time and less trouble. This marketplace distorts our ability to learn from what is happening; the marketplace does not proclaim failures. Bad news disappears; "good" news becomes "fantastic" news.

If money were paid for trumpeting the truth, organization articles and advertisements would read quite differently.

Time is only one of the many parameters we must honor when we are creating renewal. Rephrase Miss West's statement to focus on the organizational world and it might read, "If it's worth doing, it's worth doing thoughtfully." The timing, speed, and pace of change are a part of a larger context. Much that surrounds our work distracts from thoughtfulness: our impatient culture; systems that feed on today's numbers, such as the budget or the stock price; commitments others have made; and the egos of everyone involved, including our own. Since renewal efforts are out of the norm, they get exceptional attention both from those who want them to succeed and others who want them to fail. This spotlight intensifies the pressure to accelerate and deliver now.

There are models and methods allowing organizations to do in weeks what used to take them months to accomplish. These wonderful technologies allow organizations to engage hundreds of people simultaneously, collapsing the calendar time required, increasing the shared understanding and investment, and increasing the human hours invested. But to be effective, the opportunity to do more in less calendar days must still allow time for thoughtfulness.

Reflection must surround action. We must have time to step back from what we are doing, to look at it from a quieter, loftier point, removed from the madness of the moment. Renewal does not thrive under pressure; it wants to move at its own pace—which usually means years rather than weeks. Renewal wants to emerge in its own time, rather than within plans and projections. Renewal calls for reflection on and learning from all that has happened thus far, rather than reaction to the pressures of the moment.

Many people do not have time to pause, step back, and think; they work in pressure-cooker organizations that preclude this. Whether they have time to reflect is not the point. There is no resolution within the cooker. Eventually they will be forced to step out of the cooker and their pressurized experience will not have prepared them to be ready for what they need to do next: step back, breathe, and look at their work through new eyes.

Some questions for you to consider when the pressures at work come up against the pace of renewal:

- How do we assure ourselves that we are moving with a pace and intensity appropriate to our work?
- How do we help all invested parties learn more about what creating organizational renewal requires?
- Describe experiences where projects were faced with time pressures and succeeded. What can we learn from them?
- What is our response when the need for results is accelerated? How do we make it less likely we will be put in that situation?
- What will we do if this renewal project begins to take more time than we anticipated?

Assertion 20
We Make Renewal Happen Here and Now

It is happening right here, in the muddled middle of this organization . . . you and a few people around you . . . often with less than ideal timing . . . not there and then, but here and now. In fact, renewal *is* happening here and now. Put your ear to the ground and you can hear its rumblings. Everything is already in motion; it's more a matter of getting on board than of starting it up. The challenge is to understand what is happening, see what it has to do with what you hope will happen, and swing on board to influence it.

This is the scary opportunity for us. When renewal happens here and now, we can't point to someone else or wait; we have to decide what we are going to do. Our aspirations may be far in the distance, but any progress toward them will come out of what we choose to do here and now—or choose not to do. Choices visit us several times each day as we decide how to move forward in our reach for renewal.

Knowing this responsibility is both a burden and a blessing. No wonder we often ask management to take over. It can be very useful to have the support of authority and hierarchy. No doubt about it, they have the power that will get attention for your project. And there may be a part of you that would like to use their power to require everyone here to do what you want. But please don't declare them essential. Please don't say things like, "Well, if Prufrock isn't on board, we might as well forget it." Or "We are just paralyzed until the Executive Committee acts." Or "What's the point in us trying anything new, we know what she is going to say." These statements usually precede or summarize a story about the selfish, slippery, snail-like ways of management, diverting us from our opportunity to make renewal happen here and now.

When we sign up for the notion that organizational renewal doesn't start with us, here and now, but "up there with them," we choose a dependent and passive role. We disconnect our brains and disempower ourselves. And we wait on " . . . the only people around here who can do anything: the people at the top." The fact is, most change does not start at the top. Read the books and articles; look at your own experience: Most change starts out in the organization with someone like you. Then it may get the attention of an executive who elevates, promulgates, and disseminates it. Yes, everyone is now paying attention, but it didn't start with "the people at the top." And there is nothing automatically positive about getting management attention. I can think of a renewal project that was doing fine until recognized by an executive who then declared "what's good for this plant is good for the company." The project suffered and the company-wide effort failed.

The essential support for renewal comes from those of us here who want it now. When we define ourselves as powerless, we will act as if we are powerless, and our hopes will be lost in hopelessness. We decide whether to invest ourselves; we decide whether it is worth it. We may choose to involve others, expanding our network of support. We may reach out to executives for the unique support available there, but this need not be our immediate reflex. Questions for you to consider back at work include:

- ✧ Tell stories of individuals taking responsibility for making renewal happen here and now.
- ✧ What have we done together recently that demonstrates our personal commitments to making things happen here and now?
- ✧ When we put our ear to the ground, what stirrings do we hear in this organization?
- ✧ What is already going on here that we could build upon?
- ✧ What are some ways that we could use the power of the formal structure without giving up our own power?

Summary

The assertions in these last four chapters can bring new vitality and creativity to work groups. Many assertions inform every moment of your work together; a few of these twenty are always lurking behind whatever you are doing. I've summarized them here, with their questions, so you might better use them.

Twenty Renewal Assertions With Discussion Questions

1. Pursue life.

- ✧ What do we aspire to in our lives?
- ✧ How do we currently realize our life aspirations through our work?
- ✧ What is the organization reaching for that has the promise of fulfilling people's lives?
- ✧ How do our aspirations fit with the current organizational culture?
- ✧ What opportunities are there to engage people in these questions?

2. Commit to a compelling unknown.

- ✧ What is the very best outcome we hope to see from our work together?
- ✧ What could this organization attempt that would be potentially both good for the organization and exciting to the people in it?
- ✧ Individually, what do you find compelling in what you are now doing?
- ✧ Individually, describe some projects you have participated in that were especially exciting. What made them that way?
- ✧ What would a renewal effort have to contain for you to commit strongly to it?
- ✧ How can we support continued excitement about work and renewal here?

3. Take a grand leap.

- What would be truly a great and scary leap forward for this organization?
- What do people find most compelling about making this great leap?
- What frightens people about the leap?
- What could you choose to do together to prepare you for this leap?

4. Face the future ready to learn.

- How does this organization uphold the importance of learning?
- Where have we seen leaders valuing humility?
- What do we need to learn? What are our key unanswered questions?
- How might we show a readiness to learn in the midst of renewal?

5. Create irrational positive expectations.

- Describe successful work experiences in which trust and hope were essential elements.
- What does trust mean to us? How do we demonstrate it?
- How do we build trust among people who need it to work together?
- How does trust figure into our current projects?
- What is the hope or fulfillment that brings people to work each day?
- How do people hope their work here will support their lives beyond work?

6. Renewal takes root in the past.

- What are the essential values and purposes that made us what we are, without which we would cease to be?
- Which of these are most important to our future?
- How are we supporting the continuation of these from our past into our future?
- Who would be important to engage in this effort?

7. New effort relies on old resources.

- Tell stories from the old days that express what we want to have here today.
- What special experience and abilities, connections and culture, have we developed over the years?
- What from the past is important to our future?
- How could we retain and reinforce these abilities and qualities in the organization?
- What could we do to make sure our renewal efforts respect the individuals that represent the history of this place?

8. Change doesn't make sense.

- What changes are considered "nonsense" to the people whose work will be changed? How would they express that?
- What makes sense to the people working here? How would they express that?
- How does the organization appreciate its people's contributions, experience, service, and loyalty?
- How could we engage affected people in the early stages of renewal?
- What could we do to help people feel good about themselves while changes are taking place in their work?

9. We fall back on the familiar.

- ✧ What are some of the old and familiar ways of this organization?
- ✧ Describe experiences in which we relied on old ways past their usefulness.
- ✧ What are the organization's reactions when established ways are challenged?
- ✧ What are we doing to demonstrate our openness to new ways?
- ✧ How do we help people step back from the familiar to consider effectiveness?

10. We spend years preparing not to change.

- ✧ What have we made into habits in the ways we approach our work?
- ✧ How are our habits valuable to us?
- ✧ What is our reaction when people suggest we change what we've been doing for years?
- ✧ What are some examples of habits we used to have that we have replaced? What caused us to change?
- ✧ How could we reconsider work habits to make sure they serve us well?

11. There is no right answer.

- ✧ How do we describe the situation that surrounds us? What, if any, common description do we agree upon?
- ✧ How does our way of working together keep us open to information we might need?
- ✧ How do we choose? What's the process? How does it work?
- ✧ Describe experiences in which we have created good alternatives and made good choices together.
- ✧ How do we go about creating answers together?

12. Find the creative tension.

- ✧ If creative tension is defined as an important gap between what we've got and what we want, what are important gaps we are now working with?
- ✧ How do this organization's aspirations, values, or goals figure in the gaps we've got around here? What's been done to clarify the gaps with people who care?
- ✧ Tell about an experience in which this organization did a fine job of helping everyone understand a gap that needed concerted action.
- ✧ Give examples of how the gaps of various groups within this organization are different.

13. Make the complex simple.

- ✧ Give examples of projects or programs that did a wonderful job of making the complex simple. How and why were they able to do this?
- ✧ How have people in the organization reacted to past change projects? What can you learn from this?
- ✧ Select a current project and ask: What is the big picture? What are the smaller slices? What are the appropriate groups? What is the best timing?

14. Create informed choice.

- ✧ What organizational examples best demonstrate the informed choice process.
- ✧ What does the organization do best in the understanding, alternatives, choice, and commitment sequence described on page 101? And where does it most need to improve?
- ✧ Tell of work experiences where you had informed choice. How did you feel about it?
- ✧ How could we expand people's array of choices?

15. Engage everyone.

- What are the underlying assumptions about who ought to be engaged in change in your organization?
- Tell of a successful renewal experience—here or somewhere else—that engaged everyone in the organization in making change.
- How would renewal efforts currently under way be different if suddenly it was required that all affected people be involved and take action?

16. We will be asked for more than we offered.

- Describe in some detail what this organization will have to invest for this project to succeed.
- Consider large projects lasting over years: What made them more and less successful?
- Where are the points this project will most likely be seriously tested?
- What could we do to increase our acceptance of the fact that this project will be tested, will falter?
- How will we deal with others in the organization when this project is faltering?

17. Sustaining renewal is always the challenge.

- What are past examples of initiating and sustaining change efforts here?
- How do we help ourselves and others understand the differences between initiating and sustaining a change effort?
- How do our efforts in initiating a renewal effort need to differ from our efforts in sustaining it?
- What are the systems, structures, and norms of this organization that affect the renewal we wish to sustain? How might we learn more about them? How might we affect them?

18. Renewal requires loss.

- ✧ Tell stories of organizational change that involved hard sacrifice—which was worth it.
- ✧ What personal experiences have you had that involved loss and pain necessary to accomplishment or happiness?
- ✧ How could we learn more about the value of working through the painful parts of change?
- ✧ What could we do to make it more likely that people will embrace change, given that it will not be easy for them?

19. "If it's worth doing, it's worth doing slowly."

- ✧ How do we assure ourselves that we are moving with pace and intensity appropriate to our work?
- ✧ How do we help all invested parties learn more about what creating organizational renewal requires?
- ✧ Describe experiences where projects were faced with time pressures and succeeded. What can we learn from them?
- ✧ What is our response when the need for results is accelerated? How do we make it less likely we will be put in that situation?
- ✧ What will we do if this renewal project begins to take more time than we anticipated?

20. We make renewal happen here and now.

- ✧ Tell stories of individuals taking responsibility for making renewal happen here and now.
- ✧ What have we done together recently that demonstrates our personal commitments to making things happen here and now?
- ✧ When we put our ear to the ground, what stirrings do we hear in this organization?
- ✧ What is already going on here that we could build upon?
- ✧ What are some ways that we could use the power of the formal structure without giving up our own power?

Part Four

Renewing Organizations, Groups, and Individuals

If the beauty we are seeking is already present in some nascent form, how do we find it and feed it? An old joke comes to mind: A tourist in New York City asks a local man in dark glasses lounging on the street corner, "How do you get to Carnegie Hall?" and is told, "Practice, man, practice. . . . " And how do we find the beauty in the beast? Practice, man, practice. . . . The answer comes from a source different from the question. The question desires a destination; the answer declares a process. *The practice of seeking* the beauty *is the finding.* The beauty is in the dynamic of the process.

What does that mean in practical, day-to-day terms? How do we establish processes within our organizations, our work teams, and our own lives that keep us continually searching for beauty and breathing new life into organizations? In Part Three, we offered twenty assertions to deepen and maintain the dynamic. Here in Part Four, we will offer three experiences that provide glimpses of beauty in the real organizational world around us. Each chapter is an example of what could be done, rather than what should be done. The chapters all focus on actions that aspire to long life.

- **Chapter 11, "Renewing a Large Organization,"** offers a living example of renewal at work, and we will focus on the dynamic group at the center of this.
- **Chapter 12, "Bringing Work Groups to Life,"** offers five ways to breathe life into group meetings.
- **Chapter 13, "Practicing Renewal Daily,"** centers on a daily practice you could adopt to remind yourself of what you are becoming.

All three chapters describe what has worked for others. My hope is that these examples for an organization, a group, and an individual will help you come up with practices of your own. These chapters do not give the street directions to your Carnegie Hall. Instead they describe practices that others have engaged in that might help you come up with some of your own. Oh, and we probably should add the experience of Belle and the Beast: Remember that they met regularly, considered large questions, developed a relationship in the process, and lived happily ever after!

Chapter 11

Renewing a Large Organization

This chapter answers the question: How can renewal happen in a large organization? Somehow all of our wonderful ideas and aspirations must come together in action. Whether spontaneous, orchestrated, or systematized, organizations somehow converge on ways of moving and growing. Most intentional renewal efforts have a nucleus of people who concentrate and disperse the energy related to change; I'll call that group "the renewal team." This team continuously helps the larger organization understand itself in relation to the world within and around it—what it is and what it might become. The chapter focuses on the work of this vital team: roles, examples, and lessons.

The Roles of the Renewal Team

Higher organisms have a heart, brain, and central nervous system that pump life to, gather information from, and guide the larger body. This is also true for these huge organisms we call organizations; they have their own forms of heart, brain, and central nervous system. In more autocratic organisms, management performs these vital functions and assigns the other bodily functions to the rest of us. In more democratic organisms, the vital functions are more widely dispersed; various parts think, feel, and act for themselves—hopefully in concert with the larger body.

What's true for the organizations themselves is also true for the renewal teams within them. Their makeup and character tends to reflect the organism they are renewing. If they are to be successful in gaining support from the more mature organization around them, their makeup needs both to respect the current organization and to not be bound by it. "Respectful renegades" embodies the paradox of the team's existence. If they are entirely respectful, they will not likely offer anything new. If they are entirely renegades, they will lose their power within the organization that created them. In earlier days, I favored renewal teams that reflected a more revolutionary character. Now I see that what may be exciting for team members does not necessarily translate into long-term effectiveness.

The team may be a cross section of the organization by level and function, or it might be the management committee. My focus is roles, not makeup. It may be highly democratic, involving everyone at every turn, or it might be dictatorial, involving no one at any turn. The team can be entirely in the head of the top executive with four others that she tells what to do. Or team responsibility might rotate through hundreds of people over the next few years. In either case, this is the renewal team. Our choices of who is on the team and how it will operate reflect our values, but there is nothing necessarily autocratic or democratic about being engaged in renewal.

System-wide renewal efforts are seldom successfully led by an individual charging to the future, making it up as he or she goes, dragging the rest of us along. But frankly, the success rate of wider-reaching group efforts is not that great either. I favor a small group of people, around six to eight, dedicated to moving this renewal forward. They become the heart, brain, and central nervous system—yet always reliant on the rest of the body. Don't get the idea that this renewal team is the only unit responsible for this kind of thinking and doing. Other teams, departments, and managers will feel related responsibilities. In fact, the renewal team will have to sort this out over and over again as it rubs up against other units invested in change . . . or no change.

Much of the power of a renewal team comes from the roles it is assigned, the roles it takes on, and its effectiveness in carrying out those roles. This list shows many of the more common expectations renewal teams have of themselves:

- Understanding the organization's history
- Knowing what's happening in the organization now
- Expressing the aspirations of people across the organization
- Sensing what this organization needs
- Assessing the political environment
- Learning what is happening in other organizations
- Gathering information from stakeholders
- Assuring common understanding of direction
- Scanning the organization's environment
- Envisioning the organization's future
- Creating plans and steps
- Involving everyone affected
- Gaining support for new directions
- Designing meetings and events
- Leading meetings
- Following and reporting on progress
- Getting attention for the effort

The renewal team comes to life through these roles. Its knowledge of and reach into the organization needs to be vast. It includes the traditional business picture, the hard data on past, present, and future, the organization in the marketplace. But it also includes the soft data on traditions, culture, climate, norms, politics. The team intends to absorb and hold the vital information about the body it is renewing.

The Learning Group: An Example

What follows is a description of a renewal effort that incorporates many of the features described on the previous page. The description is based on over four years of work by a company in the energy industry. I have stepped back from many of the details of the process to focus you on the dynamics of "The Learning Group," a constellation of teams, at the center of this renewal effort. This is a description, not a prescription, offered to stimulate your thinking. I will elaborate on the more effective elements of the Learning Group's work; you can be sure that it didn't go as smoothly as I describe it, but it continues to be a highly effective effort. Let's begin!

Imagine the president of the company forming a Renewal Team of ten people: Eight are about evenly split—salaried and hourly, manager and worker, union and nonunion, men and women—plus two consultants, one from inside and one from outside the organization. The team started with or developed into most of the roles listed earlier in this chapter. The Renewal Team posted an announcement across the company offering people the opportunity to be involved in creating change. Many volunteered and the Renewal Team chose 40 people—we will call them "The Learning Group"—people chosen for their diversity of backgrounds and work, a cross section of the company, appropriate to the task at hand. The Renewal Team would continue at the center of this effort, forming and reforming the Learning Group and facilitating its work.

The first time the Learning Group met, the Renewal Team expressed what it saw as the purposes and possibilities for renewal. It took a long time, but eventually the larger Learning Group agreed to explore creating a more viable company as seen by workers, management, suppliers, customers, communities—all the significant stakeholders. They had not much more definition than that. Those present shared both a concern for how this company might survive in the changing energy industry and a commitment to the company. At the conclusion of the meeting, all the Learning Group did was ask the Renewal Team to continue to design and run their meetings.

After the Learning Group agreed that they were a legitimate group, wanting to do something that was good for the company and for all of its stakeholders, they talked about how they might proceed. It took two meetings of talking, complaining, imagining, and wrestling with direction for the Learning Group to decide that they needed to learn a lot more about what might be possible for the company. The group brainstormed a list of areas they might learn about and asked who was interested in learning about which areas. Through a combination of volunteering and being volunteered, the Learning Group formed smaller Task Teams and sent them out into the world to find out about experiences of other people and other companies. This became the cycle that was repeated over and over again:

- Decide what we need to learn or do.
- Select a Task Team to explore this.
- Advise that team on what is expected of them.

- Send them off on their assignment.
- The Task Team presents the results of their work back to the Learning Group.
- Decide together what to do next.

The Task Teams never decide; they just do what they agreed to do. The Learning Group grew more comfortable with time, as they realized that they determined the Task Team assignments, they advised the Task Team on their approach, and nothing important was decided by the Task Team outside the Learning Group. This allowed the Learning Group to have numerous Task Teams working simultaneously, knowing that each team's work would be brought back to the whole for discussion, decision, and action. The Renewal Team that pulled together all of the Learning Group meetings was subject to these rules too; the Learning Group gave the Renewal Team its assignments. For example, the Renewal Team was regularly asked to design and lead meetings.

Over the first few months, a project emerged that was to encompass the entire company. It involved helping all employees understand the state of the company, the state of the industry, and the need for everyone to be open to alternative approaches to doing their jobs. This project was later seen as the first of several phases. The first Learning Group put together Phase One, which brought all employees together in huge meetings to explore what was happening in the industry and what they might want to do about it. After completing this phase and recognizing there was much more to do, the Learning Group reconstituted itself. About a third of the original participants left and another third were brought on board to begin Phase Two. This was not the plan from the beginning; this is what happened in response to progress.

The new Learning Group began to shape Phase Two as the first phase was finishing. The Renewal Team brought the reconfigured group together to consider where it had been, where it was, and what it might do next. New members were integrated; new purposes (based on Phase One) were explored. Where Phase

One had focused on raising the level of concern and the need for action among people across the organization, Phase Two began to focus on local action in plants and offices. New Task Teams were formed, given guidance, and sent out to learn from workers in plants across the company. They brought what they found back to the Learning Group. This provided the basis for the Learning Group's decision to design a renewal process useful across all plants, but adaptable to each. Another set of Task Teams designed the plant renewal process; Learning Group members tried out pieces of the Task Team design. After getting Learning Group approval to move ahead, the design was taken to the plants to seek their support, alteration, and implementation.

The learning and growth and change in that company has become a model for sister companies in the larger organization it belongs to. The motivation and pride of present and former Learning Group members is evident—and this was still alive in early 2000. There is much more to this project than what I have explained, but I did not want to distract you from the underlying Renewal Team/Learning Group/Task Team dynamic. I especially like the way this company involved so many people in designing their direction. They found ways of involving at least 40 people in what is usually done by a renewal team. The Learning Group repeatedly reached out to the larger organization, involving hundreds more people. The Learning Group also reformed itself so that more and more employees had the chance to be part of it at some time.

Lessons From Renewal Team Experiences

Before considering a few lessons, look back to the twenty renewal assertions in Part Three of this book. Review those assertions with your renewal team; ask their questions of your team. Whenever an assertion leaps out at you as particularly important, take it to your team for discussion.

Here are seven lessons that affect my work with renewal teams. They have much in common with regular team-building activities, but the ideas take on special meaning when applied to a small group invested in renewal.

1. **Members.** Aim for a diversity of perspective, function, level, race, gender, and experience that reflects the makeup of the larger organization as *it aspires to be*. Ask for volunteers, making it clear that only a few can be chosen. Potential members should sense this as an opportunity. Only include people willing to make a full commitment. From the beginning, plan on rotating people through the team, giving many people the chance to take on this perspective and learning.
2. **Purpose.** What is this team uniquely responsible for doing? This is a defining, continuing question for all renewal teams, whether they recognize it or not. Forming a team like this is often a first for the organization, so it won't have experience to draw upon. When the team begins its work, you will know much less about its purpose than you will later on. Keep returning to purpose; watch it evolving, watch it deepen as the work progresses. Identity and purpose are strongly linked; a team with clear purpose has a sense of itself. Help the organization continue to fully understand and support the evolving purpose of the team.
3. **Commitment.** Give the new team an early opportunity for intensive time and work together—team building. Help team members consider what they are getting involved with, the exploratory aspects of it, the time and energy it will take. Help them discover their common commitment and how they will work toward it. This early commitment creates a bond that will serve the team well later. Too many teams skip this early step and then pay for it when differences surface at a key point in the renewal process.

4. **Priority.** Make renewal work the priority for each team member. This often means team members are assigned full time to renewal. Or perhaps renewal team work varies by phase and is negotiated. Keep the team together for a defined time with renewal as the major responsibility. The important test: Is renewal work suffering because of our regular work? This is a frequent problem and an early test of the organization's commitment to the renewal team's effort.
5. **Learning.** Pursue it, express it, and act upon it. Renewal requires new perspectives, experimentation, risk, and reflection; few organizations are noted for reinforcing these requirements. Make the need to learn explicit; build it into team processes. Ground the team in new thinking that informs decisions on what to do next. Otherwise, old thinking will replicate old decisions. Visit other organizations and see what they are doing. Invite people to your organization and learn from them. Read the literature; search the Internet. Team members usually love the practical and experience-based research. It builds the team's expertise, boosts their confidence, and helps them escape the narrowing that comes with working in the same organization for years.
6. **Performance.** Consider team performance out in the organization and back in the team when members are working together. For the team to create sustained renewal in the larger organization, it must be sustaining and renewing life within itself. Important results often take years to realize, and the team needs interim measures. The team will learn and build when it pauses to review its accomplishments. Celebration of progress will help offset the effects of setbacks, and journeys into new organizational terrain always have setbacks.

7. **Connection.** Stay in close and constant touch with the organization you are serving. Too many renewal teams intentionally or accidentally isolate themselves as they plan their work. This results in unreal and unaccepted proposals. Search for ways the team and the organization can continuously work together and learn from each other.

Chapter 12

Bringing Work Groups to Life

There is excitement in working hard to fulfill a plan; working closely with others to execute a strategy can be rewarding too. But for sheer energy generated, these accomplishments seldom compare to stepping off the edge of your present organizational map into uncharted territory. Doing so with a group of committed people is a life-altering experience. The places that are most exciting to go are those we have yet to visit. The questions that are most intriguing are those that we have yet to answer or ask. We anticipate what we will learn through this unique experience. The need for excitement, intrigue, and learning is distributed widely; it is in the hearts and minds of all the people we work with. The challenge is not so much in creating that excitement, as in releasing it.

- This is worth trying, *but I don't have a clue whether it will work.*

- ✧ We have never done anything like this before, *so why should we know what to do next?*
- ✧ What we've been doing doesn't work all that well, *so it's time to do something we don't know how to do.*
- ✧ It's important for us to try this, *even though it is very risky.*
- ✧ That's a good question, *and I love not knowing the answer to it.*

The first half of each comment offers an assessment, *and the second half opens to the unknown.* The vitality of each comment comes from the combination of known and unknown; it's this dynamic between reality and possibility that creates interest and energy. Successful and alive groups have an intuitive sense of the importance of the roots/reach, presence/ascendance dynamic. A group can work even better with the dynamic when they acknowledge and build on it.

This chapter explores five methods for engaging people more deeply with their work and with their co-workers by intentionally reaching from the reality toward the possibility. Each of these approaches relies on the life that is already there, but often unrecognized. The five methods "breathe life" into a group in the sense of filling the present body with new breath. Everything that is required for life is already in the group; these methods call it forth. These methods enliven companies and agencies, communities and churches, nations and states. I will explain their use in small groups (four to twelve people) because that is easier for me to describe and for you to visualize—and because these small groups are essential to large organizations. Much of organizational life is created or destroyed, expressed or silenced, in these small groups. A growing array of large organizational change models (The Conference Model, Open Space, Future Search, Appreciative Inquiry, Real Time Strategic Change) capitalize on the vitality sparked in the dynamic between what we know and what we have yet to discover together. Here are the five life-supporting methods we will consider here:

- Clarifying the important
- Revealing secrets
- Offering gifts
- Proclaiming the positive
- Asking intriguing questions

Throughout this book we have honored the importance of questions; this chapter continues that emphasis. Each of these methods will be offered as a series of questions. Asked at the right moment, they evoke and expand the group's expression of itself and its potential.

Clarifying the Important

Answer each of these questions, one after another:

- What is our work?
- Why is that important to us?
- And why is *that* important to us?
- And why is *that* important to us?

These "Why?" questions probe for deeper meaning and purpose. Each question moves us to another level, coming closer to the truth about the life this work holds for us. Pause to try these questions on yourself regarding a current project. See where the questions lead you. And imagine what your work group could do with them if asked at the right time.

These questions can lead a small group of co-workers toward a better mutual understanding of why they come to work each day. When they share their individual meanings with each other, they discover how much they have in common at a deeper level, at the third "why" level. We are much more united at these levels than our job descriptions could ever reflect. As we move to our deeper whys, we come closer to the mutual meanings of this work in our lives: These are the real reasons we come to work; these are the sources of energy for our work together, for organizational renewal.

Revealing Secrets

In the context of our work together:

- What do we think about, but not discuss with each other?
- What secrets are we keeping to ourselves about our work?
- What anxieties keep coming to us individually that we do not express to others?
- What work concerns do we have individually that we don't want others to know about?

We tie up energy in a silent swirl about our doubts about our work, or what we've done poorly, or can't do well, or don't know how to do, or don't want to be found out on. This hidden swirl of negative energy is not available for more constructive work. And, because we don't want anyone to know these secret concerns, we have no way to escape our feelings of being less, being wrong, being inadequate. It feels like we are condemned to carry them forever! What can be done to reduce the burden of what's being hidden?

This is a touchy area, but I am not going to pass it by just because it is sensitive. Done well and at the right time, these questions release life. Do not begin by asking the group to discuss these questions together. This is much too delicate an area; that kind of frontal assault will result in everyone shutting down and tightening up. The challenge is to find a way for people to acknowledge that there is much that is unsaid, and that this has become a burden that blocks effectiveness.

Perhaps there is a way for members of the group to acknowledge their unspoken concerns without identifying themselves. Here is a way that can work with a larger group (10 to 20 people): Suggest that they all think about the questions. Have each of them write down one secret that concerns them in relation to the group's performance. Tell them that they will not be identified, but what they write will be read to the whole group and the group will consider all it hears. Tell them all of this before asking them to do anything. Then have them write their one secret on a separate sheet of paper and drop it into a box. Ask one person to read the secrets to the whole group. When the group hears all the concerns, it can discuss what it heard and deal with the patterns.

People feel better then they discover that their individual concerns are not so individual after all! And that is what usually happens. This reduces secrecy and puts more truth on the table for all to see and use. The secrets are not secrets anymore; a new level of conversation and truth is open for the group. You can feel the new receptiveness and life when this happens. Be sensitive about opening these secrets, but do not overlook its positive possibilities.

Offering Gifts

In the work we are doing together:

- What do we do together particularly well?
- What do we enjoy doing together?
- What do we bring that would we would like to give to the larger organization? Abilities? Background? Perspective? Attitudes? Experience?
- What do we have that others in the organization could benefit from?

These questions draw out people's desire to contribute what is most unique about themselves. Think of it as gifts they would like to offer. In a receptive setting, people willingly and energetically tell you of the abilities they have developed over the years. Imagine asking everyone working in an organization of 500 to answer these questions. Imagine 500 people, or 100 groups, each noting three talents they could bring to work. Think of the hundreds of gifts available to the organization!

And how might you do this with your group? Start by presenting the questions to the group and getting their support for answering the questions. Then ask individuals to spend three minutes alone thinking about the gifts they bring and completing this statement three times: "I bring _______." When they are all ready, go around the group asking each person to share one of their three answers: "I bring . . . I bring . . . I bring. . . ." Go around the group three times with no other comments. Just listen. And afterward, talk together about what they heard and felt. This will likely open the group to answering the questions together.

Proclaiming the Positive

- When have we been especially proud of this group?
- What do we appreciate in each other?
- What have been some of our best experiences in working together?
- What do we see that gives us hope for this group? For the larger organization?
- What have we seen happen in this group that draws us together?

These questions draw out our positive thoughts and experiences; they elicit stories of appreciation for what we already have; they reduce preoccupation with the negative. When answered honestly, life begins to display itself. This is not the whole picture, but it is the side of the picture frequently neglected or crowded out by more critical voices. Those critical voices are important too, but not as likely to be the source of new life. Ask the questions; listen to the stories that come back as answers.

Asking Intriguing Questions

This last method embodies the first four. It is questions about questions:

- What questions intrigue us?
- What questions arouse our curiosity? Excitement?

- What questions keep running through our minds, over and over again?
- What are the questions that we have not answered, may never answer, but keep asking ourselves?

When offered at the right time, these types of questions can provoke some intriguing responses. Our work is too often filled with answers, rather than questions. We feel compelled to know the answers—or act like we do. We make statements, showing what we know. The above questions lead people out to the edges of what they know, close to the attractions that lie just beyond their knowledge. I watched this happen during a meeting I recently attended. The life had gone out of the meeting; there was no energy for the agenda before us. Then someone said, "Forget what we've been talking about, what we've done, what we should do. . . . In the realm we have been working, what questions are you interested in? What questions are really alive for you? What excites you?" During a few moments of silence, we collected our thoughts, and then questions started spewing from the group. With all of the questions, we could feel our excitement build. We used those questions to decide what we wanted to do next, which was a new direction that had more life for all of us.

Summary

These are just five of the many ways of breathing new life into groups; there are many others. Think about humor's place in creating life. Think about sorrow, celebration, play, mourning, ritual. For clues as to what might bring life to your organization, consider your experience in your family and other communities: What brings life to them? What are they doing when you feel especially alive? What happens out there that causes your excitement to grow? Discover what brings life to other organizations and bring that to your work. Use anything that helps your group reflect on itself, learn from that, and move forward.

Chapter 13

Practicing Renewal Daily

Organizational destinies are shaped in their quest for life—as are our own. Those organizational aspirations, assertions, and questions we read in earlier chapters apply to us as well. If we did a "search and replace" of this book, substituting the word "individual" for "organization," individual life purpose and choice would be spotlighted. We are defining ourselves in each moment, and we are surrounded by opportunities to define ourselves, whether we are aware of them or not. Work usually takes so much time that we do not stop to reflect on the opportunity to try something new, or to think about our experience differently. Our challenge is to find ways of engaging ourselves with life that are at least as compelling as work. This chapter offers a few practices that can aid that shift of perspective—practices that heighten the opportunity for personal awareness, choice, and action. Engage in this practice daily for two weeks; see what difference this reflection makes.

Twenty Personal Assertions Practice

The twenty renewal assertions from Part Three will be our primary vehicle for getting this done. Each of the twenty assertions was an exhortation or declaration of what is needed to renew an organization. We will use those assertions to both remind you of what this book has been about and to help you reflect on your own life. Each assertion will be linked to personal questions adapted from the organizational questions asked in Part Three.

Here is the simple daily practice: (1) Set aside ten minutes. (2) Scan through the twenty assertions listed below with the intent of selecting one of them. (3) Find an assertion that attracts you. (4) Respond to the questions that come with it. That's it. Approach this task loosely, not as a job to do, but more as a thought stimulator and reminder of who you are. When you are doing this reflectively and it is working, the practice will have a closer kinship to meditation or prayer than to a chore from today's "To do" list. Here are the twenty assertions; set aside ten minutes a day, select one assertion, respond to it, and make a few notes along the way:

1. Pursue life.

- ✧ What do you aspire to in your life?
- ✧ How do you currently realize these life aspirations through what you do?
- ✧ How do your aspirations fit with the world that surrounds you?
- ✧ What opportunities are there to engage important others in these questions?

2. Commit to a compelling unknown.

- What are the best outcomes you hope to see from your life?
- What could you attempt that would be potentially good for you and exciting to people around you?
- Describe some projects in your life that were especially exciting to you. What made them that way?
- What must your life work contain in order for you to commit strongly to it?

3. Take a grand leap.

- What would be a truly great and scary leap forward for you?
- What do you find most compelling about making this great leap?
- What frightens you about the leap?
- How could you decide whether to take this leap?

4. Face the future ready to learn.

- How do you uphold the importance of learning?
- Where have you demonstrated humility?
- What do you need to learn? What are your key unanswered questions?
- How might you show a readiness to learn in the midst of change?

5. Create irrational positive expectations.

- Describe successful experiences you have had in which trust and hope were essential elements.
- What does trust mean to you? How do you demonstrate it?
- What do you hope for each day of your life?
- How do you hope your work here will support your life outside of work?

6. Renewal takes root in the past.

- ✧ What are the essential values and purposes that make you what you are, without which you would cease to be?
- ✧ Which of these are most important to your future?
- ✧ How are you supporting the continuation of these from your past into your future?
- ✧ Who would be especially important to engage in this effort?

7. New effort relies on old resources.

- ✧ Recall experiences from your past that allowed you to be who you are today.
- ✧ What special experience and abilities, connections and culture, have you developed over the years?
- ✧ What from your past is especially important to your future?
- ✧ What could you do to make sure that your efforts at change build on your personal history?

8. Change doesn't make sense.

- ✧ What part of you thinks the changes you are considering making are "nonsense?" How would you express that?
- ✧ How do you appreciate yourself with all your effort, history, and patterns—whatever those might be?
- ✧ How do you ensure that the changes you are considering really make sense for you?
- ✧ What could you do to help yourself feel good about yourself while making changes in your life?

9. You fall back on the familiar.

- ✧ What are some of your old and familiar ways? Give a positive and a negative example.
- ✧ Describe experiences in which you relied on old ways past their usefulness.
- ✧ What are your reactions when your established ways are challenged?
- ✧ What are you doing to demonstrate your openness to new ways?
- ✧ How do we help people back from the familiar to consider effectiveness?

10. You spend years preparing not to change.

- ✧ What is one habit of yours, and how is it valuable to you?
- ✧ What are some examples of habits you used to have that you have dropped or replaced?
- ✧ When you have changed, what caused you to change?
- ✧ How could you reconsider your life habits to make sure they are serving you well?

11. There is no right answer.

- ✧ How does your way of working keep you open to information you might need?
- ✧ What larger purpose do you uphold that guides almost every decision you make?
- ✧ How do you choose? What is your process? Describe it.
- ✧ Describe experiences in which you have come up with good alternatives and made good choices.

12. Find the creative tension.

- ✧ If creative tension is defined as an important gap between what you've got and what you want, what are three important gaps you are now working with?
- ✧ How do your aspirations, values, or goals figure in the gaps you've identified?
- ✧ Tell about an experience in which you did a good job helping yourself and others understand a gap that needed action.
- ✧ Give examples of how the gaps you experience are different from other people's gaps.

13. Make the complex simple.

- ✧ Think through some examples of how you deal with complexity in your life.
- ✧ How do you make the complex simple for yourself and for others?
- ✧ How do people react to your simplifying of situations? What can you learn from this?

14. Create informed choice.

- ✧ Describe an experience in which you were able to make a better choice because of the array of options before you. How did you feel about that?
- ✧ How could you regularly expand people's array of options?
- ✧ What do you do when working with others to help them make better choices?
- ✧ How do you help other people build their commitment to decisions?

15. Engage everyone.

- ✧ What are your underlying assumptions about how people ought to be involved in change that affects them—whether at work, at home, or in the community?
- ✧ Tell of a successful change experience in which the key people affected were successfully involved in making change.
- ✧ How would your efforts to help others change be affected if you were suddenly required to engage everyone involved?

16. You will be asked for more than you offered.

- ✧ Consider changes you have made in yourself over the last few years: What made those changes more and less successful?
- ✧ Can you think of any changes you have undertaken that ended up taking a lot more effort than you originally intended? If so, describe one.
- ✧ What do you typically do when you find the personal change you intended requires much more effort than you had originally intended to give? Do you have patterns of doing this?
- ✧ How do you deal with others you are working with when they start giving up because of the magnitude of effort required?

17. Sustaining renewal is always the challenge.

- ✧ Describe two examples of personal change that you initiated and sustained for years.
- ✧ What is the difference for you in initiating personal change and sustaining it?
- ✧ What do you do over the long term to sustain the personal changes you wish to make?
- ✧ What and who around you helps you sustain personal change and make the new behavior part of who you are?

18. Renewal requires loss.

- What personal experiences have you had in which loss and pain accompanied success and happiness?
- What is your first response to an important loss in your life (a friend, a parent, a project, a game)? Have you noticed any patterns in how you respond to loss—whatever it might be?
- What have you learned about the pain that often accompanies change?
- What could you do to make it more likely that you will embrace change the next time it happens?

19. "If it's worth doing, it's worth doing slowly."

- How do you assure yourself that you are moving at a pace and with an intensity appropriate to your work and life?
- Recall a personal experience in which you faced time pressures and succeeded. What did you do that allowed you to succeed?
- What is your response when the time you have to complete something is sharply reduced?
- How do you make it less likely that you experience time binds in your life?

20. You make renewal happen here and now.

- Recall three times when you took responsibility for taking action here and now—rather than sitting around and waiting for someone else to make things happen.
- What have you done recently that demonstrates your commitment to making things happen here and now?
- To what extent do you automatically see other people and organizations as aids or deterrents to what you want to accomplish?
- How do you use the power of organizations (schools, companies, government, health-care *services*, etc.) to aid you in bringing about change?

See what happens when you make this exercise a daily practice, selecting a different assertion each day. Step back from your world to observe yourself within it; pause to reflect. You will get new ideas, imagine new options, discover even more to think about, and deepen your sense of yourself. The challenge is sustaining this larger perspective so it informs you moment to moment. If this exercise does not do it, find one that will. It may be daily reading, or writing in a journal, or conversation with someone with like interests. There are many practices; choose one and do it.

Our aspirations come to life in small, rather humble, daily individual actions like those suggested in this chapter—and in the two earlier chapters about organization and team efforts. In reviewing the examples of renewal practice explained in these chapters, their simplicity is apparent to me. And I know that it is through practices like these that we create the world we desire. It's the reach these practices represent that gives them a nobility—their reach for purpose, their hope, their roots in the community, and their commitment to bring renewal over time.

Conclusion: The Choices We Make

Twelve years ago I wrote a long letter to a plant manager I was working with. The letter embodied my hopes and fears for his organization's renewal. His plant was in the middle of redesigning itself, renewing the life of the workplace, and attempting to build on the plant's rich history. The project had grown well beyond its early success and was taking root in the organization. But it was beginning to bog down. While flying home from a sobering visit, I put down my thoughts. Like this book, the letter asserts the project's life-giving elements. Like this book, it expresses the struggle to reach beyond the pressures of the moment to create something to be proud of for generations.

Dear Steve,

My flight home from our meetings gave me time to remind myself of the underlying assertions we discussed a couple of years ago when this project surprised us by its leap into being. Remember our astonishment when we discovered that together we were involved in recreating this plant, not just solving pressing problems? And remember engaging more and more people in the idea, eventually getting everybody involved and committed to reshaping this place in ways consistent with the old family values, but informed by new technology, changing workforce, and a more competitive marketplace? Those were wonderful times! Well, here is some of what we were asserting then; this is a good time to remember what we are reaching for:

1. *This effort is bigger than any one of us or any number of us. We intend to put a process in place that is so compelling there is no alternative but to continue it. It must be bigger than changes in management, changes in company direction. We want to create something that everyone honors.*
2. *None of us expect to be here when this project is "completed." In fact, none of us expect it will be completed. Its life is larger and longer than our contributions.*
3. *This project is so important that even when we discover we are not succeeding with our present approach, when what we are doing is "wrong," we will learn and adjust but not consider letting go of the project. In fact, it's not a project; it's a way of life.*
4. *We intend to be very patient; we do not need to get there tomorrow. This patience informs all of our decisions. There are short-term setbacks (like we are experiencing now) that we expect, will deal with, and live through.*
5. *These new ways of working will require a huge effort, much larger than we anticipated when we were beginning. I remember discussions about what this would take and the commitment growing out of those discussions. What we are now doing is grander than we imagined, both in energy required now and potential benefit in the future. We must put this energy in if we are to succeed.*
6. *This effort requires that we be very forgiving, using each "mistake" as a learning opportunity. We don't expect to get it all right. This is new terrain; we haven't been here before; we will actively learn as we move forward. All information about how we are doing is friendly.*
7. *We are consciously building from and on the culture that has been created here over three generations. This culture deserves respect, caring, even love, for the work, the workers, and the workplace.*

8. *This organization must lean toward its potential—the vision that everyone in the plant has been involved in defining. Doing this will assure the growth of the plant and everyone in it.*
9. *A most unique aspect of this effort (compared to others I've been part of) is that we have described it as having a life of at least twelve years. This should profoundly affect all that we do within it. . . . Ties to my earlier point on patience.*
10. *We expect to show progress year to year, not day to day or week to week. This is hard to hold onto in the face of corporate pressures for more immediate results. Holding onto this longer view calls for different decisions than reacting to achieve next month's numbers. We need to remind ourselves of how we are doing on our own terms—as well as the organization's.*

I see this plant's life much like that of any individual who works here—only much longer. Like a human being, this organization grows and learns throughout its life and needs to grow in healthy, gradual ways. It does not need crash diets or injections of amphetamines that will show unsustainable, short-term results. It needs to grow from the life it already has toward the life it aspires to as expressed in the vision. That requires so much from all of us; we haven't done this before and are gradually learning how. I cannot think of anything more important for us to do.

Sincerely,
Geoff

Steve will see that letter for the first time when he reads this book. I am sorry I did not send it to him; I was afraid of how he might react to it; that was my mistake. But I kept the letter as a reminder of what this project was about and about the choices we were making and what guided our choices—not for just this one project, but for all of my work. I didn't know it at the time, but that letter was the start of this book.

This has been a book about aspiring, seeing, and choosing. Changing the world in small ways begins with how we see it, and we are choosing what to see in every moment of our lives. We choose based on our aspirations for and expectations of the world.

Our best choices are based in living aspirations, which inform our every breathing moment and are applied to the world as it greets us in whatever form we might see it—beauty or beast.

I finish this book with even greater fascination for those organizational beasts that contain the beauty I seek. Writing about them has increased my appreciation of and frustration with them. I know more of what I love and hate about them; I've struggled with how they use me and I use them; I know better what I aspire to create within them, not just for myself but especially for future generations. I hope you have benefited from sharing in my struggles and engaging in a few of your own.

The fairy tale that inspired the title of this book fits so well with the themes I have developed. You may recall in the fairy tale that its heroine, Belle, faced a fearsome choice when she met the Beast. The choice was how to see him. She chose to look through the apparent ugliness to search for the warm, loving person beneath. The whole tale hangs on this exceptional act. Because it is a fairy tale, she ends up with a handsome prince and lives happily ever after! Would that each of us had the courage to choose, to affirm Beauty, to be the Belle to our organizational Beasts. The story was written long ago and passed on to us from earlier generations. And behind the fairy tale are the life questions: What are you seeing? What are you affirming? What are you choosing? What is the tale you are writing?

Face the Beast.
Aspire to the Beauty.
Choose while engaged with both.
If there is a secret, that is it.

Related Resources

Basler, Frank. "Creating a Transforming Vision for 21st Century Organizations." Organization Development Network Proceedings, 1999. Contact BaslerAsoc@aol.com

Bellman, Geoffrey M. *The Consultant's Calling: Bringing Who You Are to What You Do.* San Francisco: Jossey-Bass, 1990. Contact http://www.josseybass.com

Bellman, Geoffrey M. *Getting Things Done When You Are Not in Charge.* San Francisco: Berrett-Koehler, 1992. Contact http://www.bkconnection.com

Bellman, Geoffrey M. *Your Signature Path: Gaining New Perspectives on Life and Work.* San Francisco: Berrett-Koehler, 1996. Contact http://www.bkconnection.com

Collins, J. C. and Pouras, J. I. *Built to Last: Successful Habits of Visionary Companies.* New York: Harper Business, 1994. Contact http://www.harpercollins.com

Cooperrider, D.L. and Srivastva, S. *Appreciative Management and Leadership: The Power of Positive Thought and Action in Organizations.* San Francisco: Jossey-Bass, 1990. Contact http://www.josseybass.com

De Gues, Arie *The Living Company: Habits for Survival in a Turbulent Business Environment.* Boston: Harvard Business School Press, 1997. Contact http://www.hbsp.harvard.edu

Holman, P. and Devane, T. *The Change Handbook: Group Methods for Shaping the Future.* San Francisco: Berrett-Koehler, 1999. Contact http://www.bkconnection.com

Korten, David. *The Post-Corporate World.* San Francisco: Kumarian Press/Berrett-Koehler, 1999. Contact http://www. bkconnection. com

Index

A
acceptance, 13–15, 32, 34
of self, 10–11
achievement, 22–24
actions, 9, 37, 48, 65
adaptation, 105–6
alternatives, 101
answers, 96–97, 119, 141, 147
appreciation, 32, 34, 39
ascendance, 49–51, 55
ascendant life, 51–52, 55
ascendant organizations, 49–50
aspirations for, 56–61
ascriptions, 76
aspirations, 39, 53–55, 78, 113, 151, 155–56
for ascendant organizations, 56–61
rewards of, 62
assertions, 73–74
twenty personal assertions, 144
change doesn't make sense, 89–91, 118, 146
commit to a compelling unknown, 77–79, 116, 145
create informed choice, 100–102, 120, 148
create irrational positive expectations, 81–84, 117, 145
engage everyone, 102–3, 121, 148
face the future ready to learn, 80–81, 117, 145

twenty personal assertions *(continued)*
find the creative tension, 97–98, 120, 148
"if it's worth doing, it's worth doing slowly", 111–13, 122, 150
make the complex simple, 98–100, 120, 148
new effort relies on old resources, 88–89, 118, 146
pursue life, 75–77, 116, 144
renewal requires loss, 109–11, 122, 150
renewal takes root in the past, 86–88, 118, 146
response to renewal, 73–74, 95–96, 103–4
sustaining renewal is always the challenge, 108–9, 121, 149
take a grand leap, 79–80, 117, 145
there is no right answer, 96–97, 119, 147
we fall back on the familiar, 91–92, 119, 147
we make renewal happen here and now, 113–15, 122, 150
we spend years preparing not to change, 92–93, 119, 147
we will be asked for more than we offered, 106–8, 121, 149
assumptions, 37–38
awareness, 32

B
beauty, xii, 35–36, 123–24
blaming, 8–9, 10–11, 17, 31
boundaries, 64
British Navy, 22
bureaucracy, 21–22
achievement and, 22–24
choice and, 30–31
coming to terms with, 32–34
complexity and, 27–29
predictability and, 24–26
stature and, 26–27

C
change, 89–91, 118, 146
loss and, 109–11
resistance to, 92–93, 119, 147
change models, 136
choice, xii–xiii, 9, 64, 90, 101, 153
bureaucracy and, 30–31
informed, 100–102, 120, 148
renewal and, 113–14
Churchill, Winston, 16
clarifying the important, 137
commitment, 101, 132
level of effort, 106–8
unknown and, 77–79, 116, 145
community, 59–60
complexity, 27–29, 98–100, 120, 148
connection, 68–69, 134
consultants, 128
continuity, 68
contribution, 38, 57
control, 10, 18–19, 22, 24, 107

corporate culture, 26, 154
corporations, 7, 8. *see also* organizations
creative tension, 97–98, 120, 148
cynicism, 30–31, 76

D

deserters, 107, 108
dilemmas, ix–x, 16–17, 25–26, 87
direction, 67
discontinuity, 68

E

effort, 88–89, 106–8, 118, 146, 154
empowerment, 101, 114–15
encouragement, 76
energy, 76
engagement, 102–3, 121, 136
excitement, 65
expectations, 8–9, 10, 16, 17, 81–84, 105
experience, 124
experimentation, 65

F

familiarity, 91–92, 119, 147
future, 38–39, 80–81, 117, 145

G

gifts, 139–40
groups. *see* learning groups; renewal teams; small groups; teams

H

habits, 92–93, 119, 147
harm, 7, 8–9
hate, 3–4, 8–10
help, 5–6, 9–10
hierarchy, 26–27
hope, 60, 81–84, 117, 145
humility, 80–81, 117, 145

I

identity, 57–58, 64, 132
imagination, 36, 39
importance, clarifying, 137
individual, 27–28, 66, 144
  aspirations and, 56–61
  patterns, 32–33
  self-perceptions, 9–11
inquiry, spirit of, 65–66
interdependence, 59
irrational positive expectations, 81–84, 117, 145

K

knowledge, 32, 100, 107

L

larger picture, 99, 154
leadership, 24–25, 67
leap of faith, 79–80, 117, 145
learning, 37, 65, 100, 112, 133, 154
  face the future ready to learn, 80–81, 117, 145
learning groups, 128–31
The Learning Group, 128–31
life
  ascendance and, 51–52, 55
  pursue life, 75–77, 116, 144
  questions for, 47–49
  signs of, 63–64, 69
life span of organizations, 41–42, 44

loss, 109–11, 122, 150
love, 5–7, 32, 34
loyalties, 86

M
members, 132
models
military, 15
organizational change models, 136
six-phase model, 32–34
two-by-two matrix, 4–5
motivation, 90

O
openness, 80–81, 97
opportunity, 60, 63
order, 18–19, 24, 25
organizational change models, 136
organizations. *see also* assertions; questions
ascendant, 49–50, 56–61
blaming, 8–9, 10–11, 31
dependence on, 13–14
dilemmas of, ix–x, 16–17, 25–26, 87
hating, 3–4, 8–10
large organizations, 124–28
life span, 41–42, 44, 154, 155
limitations, 15, 41
perspectives on, xi, 1–2, 9–10, 37, 45, 56
signs of life, 63–64, 69

P
Parkinson, C. Northcote, 22
Parkinson's Laws (Parkinson), 22
past, 38–39, 85
long-term workers, 86–87, 88–89
renewal takes root in, 86–88, 118, 146
patience, 154, 155
performance, 133
personal assertions, 144
perspectives, xi, 9–10, 37, 45, 56
positive, 81–84, 117, 140, 145
possibility, 92, 136
potential, x–xi, 8–9, 16, 59, 155
practicing renewal daily, 123, 124, 143, 151
predictability, 24–26, 37, 87, 90
present, 38–39, 95–96
renewal in, 113–15, 122
priority, 133
profit motive, 8
purpose, 56–57, 132

Q
questions, 41–44, 116–22. *see also* assertions
ascendance and, 49–52
aspirations and, 53–54
intriguing, 140–41
for life, 47–49
reframing the world with, 44–47

R
rationality, 89–91, 98–99
reach, 73
reality, 58, 73, 74, 105–6
reflection, 112
renegade image, 126

renewal, xiii, 72–73, 75. *see also* assertions
effort and, 106–8
loss and, 109–11, 122, 150
past and, 86–88, 118, 146
practicing renewal daily, 123, 124, 145, 151
in present, 113–15, 122
response to, 73–74, 95–96, 103–4
roots of, 73, 85–88, 118, 146
sustaining, 108–9, 121, 149, 151
time frame, 22, 38, 111–13, 155
renewal teams, 125–28
The Learning Team, 128–31
lessons from, 131–34
roles, 127–28
resources, 85, 88–89, 118, 146
respect, 126
response to renewal, 73–74, 95–96, 103–4
responsibility, 10–11, 64, 114–15
results, 37
risk, 76, 79–80
roots of renewal, 73, 85–88, 118, 146

S

secrets, revealing, 138–39
services, 13–15
simplification, 98–100, 120, 148
six-phase model, 32–34
skills, 105
small groups, 124, 135–37
asking intriguing questions, 140–41
clarifying the important, 137
learning groups, 128–31
offering gifts, 139–40
proclaiming the positive, 140
revealing secrets, 138–39
stature, 26–27
stewardship, 57
structures, 16–17
sustaining renewal, 108–9, 121, 149, 151

T

task teams, 128, 129–31
team building, 132
teams, 28–29. *see also* renewal teams
tension, 97–98, 120, 148
time frame, 38, 111–13, 122, 155
trust, 82–84, 117, 145
two-by-two matrix, 4–5

U

understanding, 32, 101, 103
unknown, 77–79, 116, 145

V

volunteers, 129, 132
vulnerability, 82–83

W

West, Mae, 111
work groups. *see* small groups
work process, 66–67
world, views of, 18–19
worth, 57

About the Author

Geoff Bellman has been hating and loving organizations for over thirty years. He worked inside major corporations for fourteen years before starting his own consulting business in 1977. Geoff's external consulting has focused on renewing large corporations—financial institutions, telecommunications, consulting firms, energy companies, and an occasional government agency. He now gives most of his consulting time to community organizations.

Geoff's earlier books include *The Consultant's Calling* (Jossey-Bass, 1990), *Getting Things Done When You Are Not in Charge* (Berrett-Koehler, 1992), and *Your Signature Path* (Berrett-Koehler, 1996).

Geoff belongs to the Organization Development Network and the American Society for Training and Development, and is a founding member of the Woodlands Group. He is also a founder of the Community Consulting Project, a group of Seattle area consultants and learners who give their talents to not-for-profit organizations.

Geoff grew up in the Pacific Northwest and left in the sixties after completing his graduate work at the University of Oregon. His family followed his work around the country to Denver, New Orleans, Tulsa, and Chicago. In 1981, the family and Geoff's consulting business moved to Seattle. The three children have grown and left home. Geoff and his wife, Sheila Kelly, live in sight of Puget Sound and the Olympic Mountains and are unlikely to ever move again.

You can contact Geoff at (206) 365-3212 or gbellman@aol.com